W9-BKL-168

THE COMPLETE
YOUTH GROUP CHECKUP
AND OTHER GREAT RETREATS

THE COMPLETE YOUTH GROUP CHECKUP

AND OTHER GREAT RETREATS

EDITED BY
TOM SALSGIVER

Abingdon Press
Nashville

THE COMPLETE YOUTH GROUP CHECKUP
AND OTHER GREAT RETREATS

Compilation copyright © 1992 by Abingdon Press

This book is printed on recycled, ♻ acid-free paper.

Library of Congress Cataloging-in-Publication Data

The complete youth group check up and other great retreats / edited by
  Tom Salsgiver
      p.   cm.—(Essentials for Christian youth)
    ISBN 0-687-36171-0 (alk. paper)
    1. Retreats for youth. 2. Youth—Religious life. 3. Youth—
Conduct of life. I. Salsgiver, Thomas L. II. Series.
BV4531.2.C5775   1992
269'.63-dc20

92-20505
CIP

The retreats included in this compilation are slightly adapted from *Directions in Faith*. All material is copyright Graded Press: This Is My Life, V.5, N.4, 31-34, © 1991; Deciding What Is Right and What Is Wrong, V.2, N.2, 27-30, © 1987; When It Hurts to Be Loved, V.4, N.1, 41-44, © 1988; Dealing with Stress, V.5, N.3, 31-34, © 1990; Easter Every Day, V.3, N.3, 31-34, © 1989; Get Behind Me, Satan, V.5, N.1, 39-42, © 1990; Should I Work After School? V.4, N.3, 31-34; © 1990; When Someone You Love Dies, v.4, N.4, 31-34, © 1990; Spiritual Life Retreat, V.5, N.3, 35-38, © 1990; How Can I Be Friends with Someone Who Is Locked Up? V. 4, N.3, 39-42, © 1990; Am I in the Clutches of an Ism? V.4, N.4, 39-42, © 1990; Relating to Persons with Handicapping Conditions, V.6, N.2, 41-44, © 1991; Building a Community of Trust, V.5, N.2, 31-34, © 1990; The Complete Youth Group Checkup, V.5, N.2, 39-42, © 1990; More Than Just a Game, V.3, N.4, 31-34 © 1988.

MANUFACTURED IN THE UNITED STATES OF AMERICA

CONTENTS

Introduction..7

1. This Is My Life..9

2. Deciding What Is Right and What Is Wrong...................... 15

3. When It Hurts To Be Loved...22

4. Dealing with Stress..29

5. Easter Every Day...37

6. Get Behind Me, Satan...44

7. Should I Work After School?...52

8. When Someone You Love Dies...57

9. Spiritual Life Retreat..64

10. How Can I Be Friends with Someone Who Is Locked Up?............. 71

11. Am I in the Clutches of an Ism?.....................................76

12. Relating to Persons with a Handicapping Condition........ 83

13. Building a Community of Trust..90

14. The Complete Youth Group Checkup..............................97

15. More Than Just a Game... 103

INTRODUCTION

Welcome to the wonderful world of retreats! Youth from around the world spend countless hours, numerous days, and many sleepless nights at lock-ins and retreats. Retreats are a great way for youth and youth groups to have fun and spend time in study, reflection, and planning.

The Complete Youth Group Checkup and Other Great Retreats is a collection of fifteen effective retreats which originally appeared in *Directions in Faith*. These retreats have been "youth tested" and then refined to be practical and easy to follow. Some of the retreats are planned to help your youth learn about the way you function as a group. Others will challenge youth to learn about life issues. All of the retreats have plenty of suggestions and detailed instructions.

Before you read the individual retreats and become excited about the possibilities for your youth, the following general suggestions about retreat planning may be of help to you.

Planning the Retreat

As you think about sponsoring a retreat, involve youth from the very beginning. Establish a planning team that includes youth. This will ensure that the youth have ownership in the event. Youth also have a wealth of knowledge and creative ideas. They will be able to help you plan activities that will appeal to their friends.

As you plan, make sure the purpose for your gathering is clear. For every retreat in this book, you will find a purpose statement. You may want to amend it to fit the needs of your own youth group, but it is very important to be clear about your goal. Make sure that all activities contribute to the goal you have established.

Choose facilities that fit your needs and purposes of the event. Can the goal of the retreat best be accomplished at a camp, a lock-in at the church, or a motel? It is often important to "get away" —to go to a different city or area. This ensures that people will not be "dropping in and dropping out" of the event.

Consider whether you want the participants to cook their own meals, have them catered, or go to a nearby restaurant. Part of the answer to the meal question will be budget, and the amount of money youth (or the church) want to (and are able to) spend on the retreat.

Choose a date well in advance. Have several back-up dates in case the facility you want is unavailable. Check the church calendar and the calendars of the schools where your youth attend. Sometimes conflicts are unavoidable, but planning far in advance will help avoid unnecessary conflicts.

Schedule

As you begin the plans for your retreat, make sure the schedule fits the needs of your group. The retreats in this book offer several different schedules—some are for one day, others for an overnight, a lock-in, or for weekend get aways. These schedules are only suggestions. Change, rearrange, reschedule, delete, add to them.

Be sure to make time for play and free time. Each retreat in this resource has some time built in for group building and play. Youth—like adults—need time to play. Often play is the best way to build a caring community. Be sure to use some activities that are noncompetitive. Competition can quickly alienate persons and factions within groups.

Each retreat includes suggestions for worship. Always make time for worship at retreats and lock-ins. It is important for youth to pray, to sing, and to talk about their faith. Also, many of the retreats suggest Holy Communion. Gathering around the Lord's Table is important for all Christians—especially youth.

Cost of the Event

Retreats do not have to break your youth budget. Do some creative thinking about where to have the retreat. Ask persons in your local church if they have a cabin or "hide away" that would be suitable for your gathering. Don't be afraid to ask hotels/motels and camp facilities if they give discounts for church groups. Often planning the retreat at a non-tourist time can produce considerable savings in room costs. Don't overlook other churches and buildings in your community as a place to get away.

Plan your meals and snacks carefully. Ask parents and church members to provide snacks, drinks, even meals. Sometimes adults will volunteer to go along just to prepare the meals.

As you do some long range planning, ask for money to be put in your church budget for retreats. Educate the finance committee or whoever makes monetary decisions that retreats have a specific purpose, a plan and outcomes that will help youth be better disciples of Jesus Christ. While churches may not be willing to fund just "fun" trips, if they understand the intent of your retreat, they may be more willing to provide the extra funds.

The Complete Youth Group Check Up is chock full of super ideas for retreats. However, they are just that—ideas. You can use the retreats just as they are, or you can change them, add to them, rearrange the ideas or the sequence, lengthen them or shorten them. They are for you and your youth group.

Enjoy and happy retreating!

Tom Salsgiver

1

THIS IS MY LIFE

PURPOSE: *To help youth reflect on who they are and to encourage them to discover their own personal history as a source of hope.*

This event offers senior high youth an opportunity to recognize and to celebrate the milestones in their Christian journeys and to develop a sense of God's presence in their personal histories and in their lives. They will examine their gifts and the gifts of others. They will commit themselves to continue to grow in faith.

Preparation

Talk with the youth and their parents about what the youth should bring to the retreat. Ask them to collect items that trace the youth's participation in the life of the church: baptism and/or confirmation certificates, old Sunday school papers, artwork, bulletins from Christmas pageants, and so forth. Ask the parents to prepare either a tape recording or written notes describing what they remember of their youths' baptism. Each youth should also bring a Bible.

Look through snapshots saved by your church and photocopy any that picture the youth in your group. Photocopy bulletins from their dramatic endeavors: musicals, dramas, Sunday school pageants and programs. Be sensitive to those youth who do not live with both parents and those whose families have joined the congregation recently. Notes from grandparents or other family members may be appropriate. Memorabilia from involvement in other churches the youth have attended should be welcomed.

Make a copy of "Discovering My Gifts" for each youth. Bring to the retreat a ream of paper, a tape recorder, and tape recordings of mood music.

Student participation in leading the retreat is important. Ask two or more members of the youth group to lead some part of the retreat. You may want to ask for volunteers or have the group select student leaders. Consider which parts of the retreat could effectively be led by members of the youth group. (For example, the "Happygram" activity, "Draw a Wish for You," reading the scripture for Evening Watch, leading the closing worship.) Hold a brief planning session with the student leaders.

POSSIBLE SCHEDULE (1 Day)

11:30 Arrive and help with lunch
12:00 Lunch, cleanup
 1:30 Make Scrapbooks
 2:30 Discovering My Gifts, (Chart Spiritual Journeys)
 3:20 Give Happygrams
 3:45 Recreation: picture charades, touch football, volleyball
 5:00 Draw a Wish for You
 5:20 Evening Watch
 5:45 Dinner, cleanup
 6:30 Celebrate the Significant Moments
 8:00 Make Covenants
 7:30 Closing Worship
 8:15 Departure

Activities

Make Scrapbooks

For this activity, the youth will need the memorabilia they brought from home. Set out on a table the extra pictures and bulletins that you brought. Provide glue, construction paper, and scissors. Give each youth a spiral notebook. Ask the youth to paste in their notebooks papers, pictures, documents, bulletins and snapshots that help them remember their participation in the church. Encourage the youth to reminisce as they make their scrapbooks. If someone has no photographs, suggest that he or she draw pictures or cartoons about big events in his or her church life.

As the youth work, ask each to tell about an important event in his or her life. Ask:

● Did the event have religious significance?
● Did it contribute to your personal growth?
● What have been important times in your spiritual life?

Play the tape recordings or read the notes that parents prepared to tell about their youths' baptism.

Discovering My Gifts

Check all the items that describe you.

_____ I enjoy belonging to organizations.

_____ I give myself time for exercise and rest.

_____ I set goals for myself.

_____ I need to win.

_____ I prefer to cooperate.

_____ I like challenges.

_____ I like to do my best.

_____ I enjoy preparing and eating food.

_____ I enjoy being male or being female.

_____ I need to belong to people.

_____ I am my own person.

_____ I enjoy the rewards of success.

_____ I want to own physical things.

_____ I need to get things done.

_____ I am easy-going.

_____ I am organized.

_____ I enjoy learning.

_____ I need to know that my future is secure.

_____ I dislike taking risks.

_____ I relate well to others.

_____ I enjoy change.

_____ I look for the unique.

_____ I need to serve others.

After the youth have completed the checklist, ask them to write a paragraph describing their qualities—for example, "I enjoy the unique and I enjoy learning and I need to feel respected . . ." Ask volunteers to read their paragraphs.

Chart Spiritual Journeys

Distribute paper and pencils. Have the youth write down times in their lives that were turning points, times of change and growth, such as when a close family member died, when they had to assume new responsibilities, when they participated in church or school projects, when they moved. Then ask them to write down signs of hope in their lives, such as college or career opportunities or new friendships. Have each youth make a graph describing his or her spiritual journey. The graph should show highs and lows, turning points, growth points, and signs of hope. When all the youth have completed their graphs, ask: What have been the most significant times in your life? Who are the other people who have been responsible for growth and for hope in your life? In what ways has God been a part of your life?

Give Happygrams

Ask the youth to sit in a circle. Distribute paper and pencils. Ask each youth to sign his or her name on the top of the paper. Collect the papers and redistribute them so that nobody has the paper with his or her name on it. Each youth is to write a positive statement about the person whose name is at the top of the paper and then pass the paper to the next person in the circle. After all the youth have written on all the papers, collect the papers and return them to the people whose names appear on them. Allow the youth time to read their happygrams. Play soft music while the youth write and read their happygrams.

Draw a Wish for You

Give each youth a paper plate. Each youth is to sign his or her name on the plate. Collect the plates and then redistribute them so that nobody has the plate with his or her name on it.

Ask each youth to draw on the plate a prayer or a wish for the person whose name is on the plate. For instance, the youth might draw a heart for love, a stick figure family for family time, a blue ribbon for an award. When all the drawings are complete, collect the plates and return them to the people whose names appear on them.

Evening Watch

Read **Romans 12:3-8, 1 Corinthians 12:28-31,** and **Ephesians 4:7-13.**
Ask:

- Which gift have you never heard of before?
- Which gift do you have? Which would you like to have?
- Which gifts do others in the group have?
- What gifts, in addition to those mentioned in the Scripture readings, do you see in yourself or in other youth in the group?

Ask the youth to choose one gift that they see in themselves and to reflect on ways God might want them to use the gift. Invite them to ask for God's direction and to pray that God might use them as part of God's work in the world.

Have a volunteer tell the group his or her gift. Ask the group: How could God use his or her gift? In what ways does his or her gift build up the body of Christ? In what ways could you enhance or contribute to his or her gift? Say a brief prayer asking God to use him or her as part of God's work in the world.

Conclude the evening watch by inviting the youth to read or sing "Spirit of the Living God."

Celebrate Significant Moments

After dinner, ask the youth to put their chairs in a circle. Invite them to sing one of the following songs:"Seek Ye First," "Alleluia," or "Jesu, Jesu." Ask: What during the retreat brought you closer to God? What brought you closer to one another?

Make Covenants

Have the group brainstorm to make a list of answers to the question: Where do we go from here? Possible answers might be these: home, back to school, to a new understanding of ourselves, to tell others about what we believe. Write the question and the answers on a chalkboard or on a large sheet of paper.

Ask the group to write a covenant. Begin by asking the youth what is, has been, or will be most important in their lives. List their responses on a chalkboard or on a large sheet of paper. Then ask: What should we, as a group, do so that our actions reflect what we say is important? List responses. Have the group dictate a covenant. It might read:

YOUTH GROUP COVENANT

Because we think that _____ is important, we will _____ .

The youth may want to write their own personal covenants. If so, provide envelopes for the youth to address so that the covenants can be mailed to them a month later.

†   Closing Worship   †

Print the following incomplete sentences on a chalkboard or a large sheet of paper. Ask the youth to fill in the blanks. Then invite the youth to read the prayer responsively.

LEADER: We believe in _____ .
GROUP: *Because we believe, we* _____ .
LEADER: We came here to _____ .
GROUP: *We leave here ready to* _____ .
LEADER: We feel God's call to _____ .
GROUP: *We are* _____ . (Here the youth may say their names.)
LEADER: We call God by name.
GROUP: *We affirm God's direction in our lives in sorrow, joy, growth, struggle, pain, love, suffering, and happiness.*
LEADER: We praise the God of history, who gives us perspective and direction.
GROUP: *We are* _____ .
(names)

Many of us were children in the church. We all are youth in the church.
LEADER: Praise God for the people who at our baptism promised to sustain us in the faith.
GROUP: *We will one day be adults in the church.*
LEADER: Inspire us; water the seeds of your spirit so that we may grow and flourish. O Creator, refresh, renew, create us as disciples.
GROUP: *We remember those who have gone before us in the church of Jesus Christ and in our church. Amen.*

Ask the group to read their covenant. Invite the group to sing "Fill My Cup" or "Seek Ye First" and then to join hands for a benediction. The youth leader or one of the youth may give the benediction. If a youth is to offer the benediction, be sure to invite someone at the beginning of the retreat so they will not be caught off guard.

—Jenni Douglas

14

2

DECIDING WHAT IS RIGHT AND WHAT IS WRONG

PURPOSE: *To help youth choose between right and wrong concerning the issues that confront them.*

A retreat can be a great way of focusing on a theme and developing corresponding skills. This retreat, with its thrust on making ethical decisions, is a good example.

Preparation

Form a planning committee. The officers of your group may compose this committee. Also include adult counselors. A youth should serve as chairperson. Identify which youth or adult will lead each part of the retreat.

Checklist

a pad of newsprint (an easel pad is best)
a tablet of notebook paper
a ball of string
masking tape
song books or sheets
pencils for everybody
tape player and cassette tapes of popular songs (ask youth to lend these items)
special food items (see "Group Building Activities," #1)
colored beads (one for each youth)
one pair of scissors
three or four felt-tipped markers
extra Bibles
old newspapers (optional)

Find out what cleaning materials are supplied by the retreat location. Usually the cleanup committee should plan on providing trash bags.

POSSIBLE SCHEDULE (2 Day)

SATURDAY
    9:30 Arrive at retreat site and settle in
   10:15 Group building activity
   10:45 Explore difficulties in making decisions
   11:30 Lunch
    1:00 Recreational activity
    1:30 Identify values that influence decision making (Part 1)
    2:15 Free time
    3:00 Group building activity
    3:30 Identify values that influence decision making (Part 2)
    4:15 Informal reflection: What has been good so far? What hasn't?
           What should we change in the remaining schedule?
    5:00 Supper
    6:30 Group building activity
    7:00 Explore strategies for decision making
    7:45 Break
    8:15 "Song-ercise"
    9:00 Free time (several different games, a movie, or a night hike)
   11:00 Student devotions
   12:00 Lights out

SUNDAY
    8:15 Breakfast
    9:30 Student devotions
   10:00 Affirm decision making skills
   10:45 Break
   11:15 Worship celebration
   12:00 Lunch, clean up

Group Building Activities

#1: *"What are you most like?"* Have four different candy bars, four different cookies, and a can of fruit cocktail. Starting first with the candy bars, instruct youth to go to a designated section of the area for the item that best describes them. For example, "Which are you most like: a Milky Way, a Three Musketeers, a Mars Bar, or a Baby Ruth?" (With the fruit cocktail, mention four of the ingredients—cherries, pineapples, pear, and peaches.) After each round, ask why the youth chose their different groups.

#2: *"Pyramid building."* According to the size of your group, form teams suitable for building a human "pyramid." (Six is a good number, with three on the bottom, two in the middle, and one on top.) Give the teams time to organize, then have them build their pyramids. (You could make this a contest, and offer a small prize to the group that stands the longest.) Afterward, note that the pyramids were organized according to their members' size and strength. As a group, similarly, God has given us different talents. When we use them, we can "stand" as a youth fellowship.

#3: *"Tied Together."* Have the youth pair off, giving each pair a piece of string approximately eighteen inches long. Instruct partners to tie themselves together at the leg. Have the teams form a line, and tell them to do different things while tied together: walk to a certain point; skip; twist. When finished, ask how they felt as they did this activity. Reflect that just as things went better when they cooperated with their partner, so the youth group will be stronger when members work together as a team.

"Song-ercise"

Play the collected cassettes of popular songs during the "song-ercise." After each song, ask for its theme. Think about how the song's theme compares to the list of values compiled under "Values That Influence Decision Making, Part 1."

Program Activities

These activities are spread throughout the retreat (see schedule). You may combine or adapt them to fit to your time frame.

Difficulties in Making Decisions

Divide the youth into two groups. Give to each group one of the following stories:
Brenda and Debbie are close friends. They grew up together. They tell each other their deepest secrets. They agreed about everything, until they went to the party. The party was held in the home of a classmate while the parents were away. Some of the guests were drinking heavily. One person offered Brenda and Debbie a beer. Brenda declined but, much to her friend's surprise, Debbie accepted. A few days later they talked about it.

Andy and Carl are in their last semester of high school. They recently turned eighteen. Andy, feeling it was his duty, registered for the selective service. Carl, however, chose not to register. He objected to war of any sort, and being in the service might force him to participate in a war. One evening the two men were talking and the subject of the draft arose. Both were surprised at their conflicting decisions.

Write the following questions on newsprint and instruct the groups to discuss them.

- What reasons will each person give for her or his decision?
- Which person do you agree with? Why?

After a few minutes, convene the groups. Have someone from each team report the possible reasons that justify the actions of the characters in their story. Then ask: "If you were confronted by situations like the ones facing these characters, how would you decide between the reasons you heard? How difficult would it be? Why?"

Follow by saying: "As teenagers, we are faced with decisions that are not always clear-cut. Let us think about some of these decisions." Make a list of the issues on a sheet of newsprint. Either ask youth for suggestions, or pass out old newspapers and ask youth to glance over them. The headlines may suggest relevant issues. Some difficult decisions include sex and dating; violence; money and possessions; single versus married lifestyle; choosing a job.

Tape the finished list to the wall. Conclude by saying, "We will deal with a few of these issues this weekend. The next time we get together, we will look at some of the values we have and how we got them."

Values That Influence Decision Making, Part 1

The emphasis of this section is on determining the values that may help us decide between right and wrong. A *value* is a principle or standard that a person believes is true. Values shape a person's lifestyle and outlook. "Value statements," as used in this section, are sentences that express the standards by which one lives.

Write the following words on a sheet of newsprint:

Bible   Church   Experience   Reason

Explain that we may obtain our values from one or more of these four ways. The following exercise is designed to give us practice in using the first three paths.

Divide into three teams. Assign to each team one of the following categories: Bible, church, experience. Have printed the following directions and give them to the appropriate team:

Bible group: Think of places in the Bible that tell us what is right or wrong. Some verses to start with are **Exodus 20:1-17** (The Ten Commandments); **Micah 6:8** (justice); **Matthew 5:21-48** (The Sermon on the Mount).

Church group: Think of the things you have heard in church: sermons; lessons by church school teachers; conversations with a pastor or another leader. Review the activities and ministries (programs) your church participates in. Discuss these programs with others in the group. Then look at the list of decisions facing us that we made in our last session. What value statement can we make? (*It is right to value human life.*)

Experience group: Group members should talk about times when they had to make difficult decisions. As they do so, ask them to tell about the advice they got from others (parents, teachers, friends) that either helped or hindered them. What values did these people use?

Give each team a sheet a newsprint. As they follow their instructions, ask them to compile a list of sentences that begin with, "It is right to . . ."

Tape the sheets on the wall when the groups are finished, and have the youth silently study them. Allow time for questions about the statements. Then discuss the following questions:

● Do you agree with all these values? If not, which ones do you disagree with and why?
● How helpful are these statements in making decisions about what is right or wrong?

Conclude by saying that we have not dealt with the most important value of all. We shall study it the next time.

Values That Influence Decision Making, Part 2

A distinctive emphasis of Christianity is its stress on freedom from rigid obedience to laws and rules. This freedom, though, is balanced by loyalty to Christ and a responsibility to serve others. Responsible freedom helps in decision making, particularly in placing values in order of priority.

Begin by showing the limits of following laws blindly. Divide into two teams and assign the following situations. Instruct each team to find a solution and dramatize it.

Group One: A few minutes ago a friend ran into your house, fleeing a street gang who was going to kill him. He needed refuge, and you hid him in a closet. Now the leader of the gang has knocked at your door. He asks if your friend is inside. What do you say?

Group Two: You are a pastor in Germany during World War II, and you are attending a meeting of the German underground. They are plotting to kill Hitler. The leader turns to you and asks for help in the assassination. What do you say?

The philosopher Immanual Kant posed the first situation. He believed that you should always obey moral rules and thus should report your friend. The second situation was similar to one that Dietrich Bonhoeffer, the theologian and pastor, faced. Bonhoeffer joined the plot.

After the presentations, ask youth to identify the conflicting values. When they have finished, ask for them to suggest how to decide.

Turn next to the Bible. Say: "At one time Paul was with people who believed that we had to live strictly by written rules. He said to them, though, that Christ has freed us from these rules. Now we are free to live *for* others. Listen to his words." Have someone read Galatians 5:13-15.

Follow by saying: "Paul has given us another value: It is right to make decisions that will help others, even if that decision may break certain rules." Use the following questions for discussion:

- Think of the decisions facing us (refer to newsprint). In what ways may Paul's thought help us resolve these dilemmas?
- Do such values have any danger?

Conclude by reading Paul's final words in **Galatians 5:22-25.** Say that although making some decisions are difficult, our goal is these "fruits of the Spirit."

Strategies for Decision Making

Review the newsprint containing key issues that you made in the "Difficulties in Making Decisions" section. Pick out, or have the group pick out, four of these. Divide into four sections, and give each section one of the issues.

Tell the groups to put themselves in the shoes of someone for whom their assigned topic is extremely important (such as a teenager who is thinking about dropping out of school, using alcohol or illegal drugs, running away from home, or having an abortion). Once youth have imagined such a situation, ask them to describe how that person may go about reaching a decision. Have each group leader write this description on a sheet of newsprint.

When the teams are finished, allow time to compare and contrast the ideas. Follow by asking for a consensus as to what elements a strategy should include. A strategy may include the following:

Become aware of the different sides of the issue.

Identify and prioritize values related to the issue by looking at one's own experiences; seeking the advice of friends, parents, teachers, and church leaders; studying the Bible and devotional material; praying.

Acknowledge the possible consequences of your decision.

After making your decision, continue to think about it and be open for change.

Put the group's strategy on newsprint, then discuss it.

- Is such a strategy practical? Why or why not?
- Do we have shortcuts when decisions have to made quickly (such as deciding about drinking at a party)? What parts of the strategy would be most important?

Decision Making Skills

This final program section ties together and affirms the skills youth have developed in making decisions. Begin by dividing into three teams. Assign to each team one of the following situations and issues:

Situation: Sally and Bob are in the back seat of a car.

Issue: How "far" should they go?

Situation: Charlie discovers his long-time friend, Clyde, has been selling drugs.

Issue: What should Charlie do?

Situation: Carol has received two job offers. One is a low paying job in a family services office and she likes that kind of work. The other is a higher paying sales job in a department store.

Issue: Which job should she take?

Instruct the group to discuss the situations, using the values and strategies formulated in earlier situations and decide on a solution. When they have decided, have them dramatize the scene. (They may describe the situations and solutions if time is limited.)

After each team finishes its presentation, ask these questions:

20

● What values did you discuss to reach a decision?
● How did the team decide which values were most important?
● What other factors influenced the decision?

When all teams have reported, recall the earlier strategy of decision making (see last section). Ask if they followed the steps in that strategy. In light of these dramatizations or descriptions, should you amend that strategy?

†   Closing Worship   †

Praise: Begin in a circle and sing some favorite devotional songs. If your group does not sing, play a couple of songs or hymns on a tape recorder.

Confession and Pardon: Pass out Bibles and turn to Psalm 51. Note that we have been dealing with making tough decisions this weekend. No matter how good we are, we make mistakes—especially when we have to decide between difficult choices. In silence ask youth to reflect on difficult decisions they have made in the past. After a few minutes go around the circle and have group members read sections of the psalm aloud.

Proclamation: Direct attention to the different sheets of newsprint, starting with the sheet listing difficult decisions. Ask youth to reflect on the events of the retreat. Use questions such as the following:

What was the most surprising thing you have learned in this retreat?

What most helped you think about deciding between right and wrong?

Consecration: In the middle of the circle place a bowl of colored beads, one for each youth. Have a youth read Luke 22:39-44. Explain that in this passage Jesus is struggling with a difficult decision: Should he face the cross? The drops of sweat symbolize the tough decisions we each have to make. Tell youth to think of one such struggle currently facing them. As they do so, have each person take a bead. When each youth has a bead, allow time for talking about these situations. Conclude with a circle prayer, in which youth pray for help in making decisions.

—Gregory Weeks

3

WHEN IT HURTS TO BE LOVED

PURPOSE: *To give youth an opportunity to understand and deal with the pain that results from stress, neglect and abuse in all families.*

This retreat is designed to help your youth deal with a sensitive and difficult issue that touches all families to some degree—neglect and abuse. During this retreat your youth will have the opportunity to understand that families are systems in which each member is affected by what the other members do or do not do. They will have the opportunity to learn that neglect and abuse are not conditions that exist in only some families, but are present to some degree in all families. They will have the opportunity to express their concerns and receive support in CareGivers groups and have the option of continuing support after the retreat.

Preparation

Setting: Schedule this retreat for a setting away from the church. You will need one large room for total group exercises and space for small groups of eight to meet in private.

Publicity: You want to make it clear that this is not just a retreat for abused or neglected kids, but for all kids. Meet with the parents in advance to carefully go over what you will be doing and deal with any fears. Stress the positive nature of the retreat—that you will be teaching kids how to support each other. You might want to include parents in the retreat and provide separate parents groups that go through the same material.

Registration: Make sure that registration forms, medical releases, and all money is turned in one week before the retreat.

Sponsors & Counselors: You will need one adult group leader for every eight youth who attend the retreat. Balance your ratio of male and female counselors with the male/female ratio of the youth so that you have adequate cabin counselors. Adult counselors should be sensitive and good facilitators. They should be good listeners. Provide advanced training for your adults. You could lead the adults through one or more of the CareGivers sessions. In this way you could model the skills you want your adults to use. Make sure that you go over the schedule, rules, responsibilities, and expectations with your adult team.

Read over the schedule and modify it to fit your group and your goals. You'll need the following supplies: food supplies, recreation supplies, large sheets of paper, markers, pencils and paper, and a ''Gray Skull'' prop for each group.

POSSIBLE SCHEDULE (2 days)

FRIDAY EVENING

    6:00 Arrive at retreat site, unload, get settled

    6:30 Games and Singing

    7:00 Orientation Session/First CareGivers Meeting

    8:30 Snack Break

    9:00 CareGivers #2: Strengths & Weaknesses of Our Family

    10:30 Break

    11:00 Worship

    11:45 Prepare for bed

    12:30 Lights out

SATURDAY

    7:30 Rise

    8:00 Breakfast

    8:30 Total Group Experience: What Is Neglect & Abuse?

    9:00 CareGivers #3: Dear Abby

    10:30 Break

    11:00 Recreation: Active Outdoor games

    12:00 Lunch

    1:00 CareGivers #4: The Power of Gray Skull

    2:30 Break

    3:00 Journey to a Special Place

    5:00 Dinner

    6:00 CareGivers #5: Healing Exercise

    8:00 Worship: James 5:13-16 & 1 Corinthians 13:4-8; The Wall of Hope

    9:00 Pack & Leave

Games and Singing

After your group arrives and gets settled in, begin with games. Start with very active games. After the games, use music to slow down the pace and prepare the group for the orientation session. Good songs might include: "They'll Know We Are Christians By Our Love," and "Pass It On."

Orientation Session

Welcome everyone, introduce the leaders and any visitors. Go over the rules in a way that is fun but also assures youth that the rules will apply to everyone. Go over the theme and schedule so that everyone knows what is planned. It is important that everyone knows when and where all activities will be located.

The Wall of Pain: Introduce the Wall of Pain by talking briefly about the Wailing Wall in Jerusalem, the only part of the Temple where the Jewish people go to pray and mourn their sufferings. Let the group know that in the same way you will have a graffiti wall on which the group can write their concerns, complaints, things that bother them, and so forth.

You might want to play a song in the background that expresses hurt in relationships as you allow youth a few minutes to write on the Wall of Pain. "The King of Pain" by the rock group The Police or some other contemporary song might be used. Let them know that they can continue to write on the Wall of Pain for the entire weekend and that at the end of the retreat they will be using this wall in the closing worship service.

Insider/Outsider: Have the group sit in a large circle with a smaller circle of empty chairs in the center. There should be enough empty chairs for about 25% of your group. Give the following explanation to your group: an insider is one who knows what is going on, who is knowledgeable about the topic being discussed, and therefore has something to say. An outsider is one who does not know much and has little to say. During the exercise those who consider themselves to be insiders will move to the chairs in the center of the circle and will discuss the topic. Those outside the circle will listen. Then the two groups will exchange places and the outsiders will discuss the topic while the insiders listen. Topics should include the following:

- What is neglect and abuse in the family? What are some examples of each?
- Is neglect and abuse present in all families to some degree? Explain your answer.
- What causes neglect and abuse in the family?
- What do neglect and abuse do to those who experience them?

As each group discusses each topic, record the responses on a large sheet of paper. Guide the discussion yourself to make sure that each person gets a chance to express their thoughts and feelings and to ask questions of the other group.

CareGivers

Divide the group into the CareGivers with about eight youth and an adult leader in each one. Have each group go to a location where they have some privacy.

Begin by going around the circle and having each person introduce themselves to the group. Have them tell one thing they like about their family and one thing they dislike about their family. Go around the circle again, this time have everyone share a time they feel neglected or abused by their family. Briefly have the group describe their hopes and fears for the weekend: why they came, what they hope will happen, what they fear might happen. Read the following guidelines for the CareGivers and have the group make a covenant expressing what they need from each other if they are to share openly and honestly within this group for the duration of the retreat.

24

Guidelines for CareGivers

1. No one will be forced to share.
2. Everyone will be encouraged to share—openly and honestly about their own experiences and views.
3. We will listen when someone is sharing.
4. We will attempt to understand what a person is saying, not solve the problem for them.
5. What is said in this group remains confidential.

Close with a circle prayer in which everyone finishes the sentence: "Lord, for this event I pray . . ."

The Web of Love

Bring the CareGivers back into the large room. Have each group of CareGivers sit in a tight circle. Each group has a ball of yarn. The first person wraps the yarn around her wrist then tosses the ball to another person in the group as they say, "I love you because . . ." and finish the sentence.

The process is repeated over and over until every person in the group is tied to every other person in the group. Make sure that each person wraps the yarn around his or her wrist.

Have the members of each group number off (1, 2, 3, and so forth). As you give the instructions to each number, that person is to do what you say with their hands. Allow several seconds for each of the following activities to be expressed:

1. Express anger.
2. Express love.
3. Try to withdraw from your CareGivers family.
4. Try to reach out to only one member of your family.
5. Express neglect.
6. Express abuse.
7. Have an adult take a pair of scissors and cut themselves out of the CareGivers family (divorce or death).

Have the groups briefly discuss what happened using the following questions:

● What happened when you did your activity?
● What similarities do you see in this exercise and the way families are tied to each other?
● Which one of the activities is close to something that has happened in your family?
● What have you learned from this exercise?

Briefly explain to the groups that many modern psychologists and counselors now think of families as systems in which everyone is tied to everyone else. Everything one member of the family does has some effect on everyone else.

Hand out pencils and paper and have everyone draw their family around the dinner table. Don't give any more explicit instructions. Let each person interpret what this means for him or her. After the youth have finished, they are to list three strengths and three weaknesses of their family. Allow a few minutes for the group to complete the exercises and then have the members share their drawings. Encourage the other members of the group to ask questions of clarification.

● What do you learn about the family from the drawing?
● Where are the points of stress in this family?

Worship

Set up for worship by turning out the lights and having enough candles lit so that everyone can see. Have one extra candle to use in the worship service.

Begin by singing a few familiar songs of hope and faith. Have a member of the group lead in prayer thanking God for those who love us and for the love that we have experienced.

Read **Ephesians 5:21-28, 6:1-4.**

Have three or four youth be prepared to speak briefly and positively about what it means to be loved and what it means to be in a family. Close the time of sharing yourself and give a summary of what you have heard.

Have a youth invite the members to share any joys or concerns they have. After each joy or concern, the whole group is to respond: "Hear our prayer, O Lord." For the closing prayer, light the extra candle and explain that you will be passing the candle around the circle. As the candle comes to each person, they are to complete the sentence prayer: "Lord, for myself this weekend, I ask . . ." and then pass the candle on. Close with a favorite Bible verse.

Total Group Experience

Begin with a brief game and then use a couple of songs to prepare the group for this session.

Have the members divide into their CareGivers and form circles. The adults in each group will lead this exercise. Each group is to brainstorm examples of abuse and neglect—from the most mild to the most extreme. As they do this, they are to divide them into acceptable and unacceptable. The idea is to see what is acceptable to each person. One family system may find a behavior acceptable while another finds it unacceptable. Write the following diagram on a large sheet of paper:

	Abuse	**Neglect**
Acceptable:		
Unacceptable:		

After you have finished brainstorming, have the group debate any of the examples. They may want to argue about whether a particular behavior or attitude is acceptable or unacceptable, or whether it is abuse or neglect—or neither.

When you've finished, point out that there are some things that we have to live with, but we don't have to like them. Some situations seem impossible to change, yet there may be things we can do to alter the situation.

Dear Abby...

Set up the "Dear Abby" letters. Each person is to write a Dear Abby letter that deals with a situation in their family that they want changed. They are to express as clearly as they can what the situation is, how they feel about it, and what they would like to see happen. Then they are to write a response from Dear Abby that expresses what they think Abby would say to their letter if they really sent it in.

After the letters have been written, close with a prayer.

CareGivers #3

Begin with an attitude check. Ask how everyone is doing so far on the retreat. What are the highs and lows of the weekend so far?

Ask the group what it was like writing the Dear Abby letters and the responses. Take a few minutes to process the experience of writing, and then ask for volunteers to share what they have written. As each person shares, the others are to try to understand the issue, what the person is experiencing, and what they want to happen. The group can give support and care. At this point do not try to come up with solutions, just try to understand the issue, what the person is experiencing, and what they want to happen. The group can give support and care. At this point do not try to come up with solutions, just try to understand the issue and the person's feelings. Continue to do this with the other members of the group as long as time allows and close with prayer.

Recreation

Make sure your recreation is extremely active. Your group members have been doing a lot of sitting and heavy processing. They need to exert energy and relieve tension. Use outdoor games that demand a lot of running.

CareGivers #4

Continue with the Dear Abby letters until everyone in the group has had an opportunity to share what they have written.

Introduce the "Power of Gray Skull." Have a prop (gray skull) ready that represents the power to change situations. Think of the prop as representing the power of God in our lives. Have volunteers ready to go first, then begin by handing the prop to a member of the group and have them reflect on the issue they raised in their Dear Abby letter.

Use the following questions as a guide:

● What would you change?
● How would things be different if this change took place?
  (It would change from . . . . . .)
● How would your life be different if this happened?
● What can YOU do to help make this happen in your family?
● What can our CareGivers group do to help and support you?

Repeat the process with other members in the group for as long as time allows. Close with a prayer.

CareGivers #5

For this exercise you will need a large sheet of paper (18" by 24") for each person in the group. These are the paper bricks that you will use to build a Wall of Hope over the Wall of Pain. Have the group form a circle and each person write his or her name on the brick with large letters. Then pass the bricks one person to the left. Each person is to write on the brick what he or she would like to say to this person in light of what has happened this weekend. They may want to share how this person has touched their life, special memories of the weekend, special concerns, hopes, and prayers for the person. Repeat the process until everyone has written on each brick.

†   Closing Worship   †

Begin with songs and an opening prayer that expresses thanks to God for the weekend. Have someone read **James 5:13-16** and **1 Corinthians 13:4-8**. Have two or three youth share what they have learned during the course of the retreat and what they can take home with them. Invite others to share, too. Have a communion service in which each person can place their brick on the Wall of Pain so that as the communion service progresses, the Wall of Pain gradually becomes a Wall of Hope. End with a song and a closing prayer led by one of the youth. (Be sure to ask someone ahead of time.)

*Note:*Consider the possibility of the CareGivers continuing to meet after you return home. You may also want to get together with the other adults who participated in the retreat to see if there are any issues that emerged that need to be addressed.

—Walt Marcum

4

DEALING WITH STRESS

PURPOSE: *To identify the nature and the cause of stress and to develop appropriate ways of responding to life's pressures.*

This event is divided into two sections. In Part 1, the group will explore the definition and the causes of stress as well as its effect on them. In Part 2, the group will focus on ways to live with stress, without falling victim to it. Take a break for refreshments at the end of Part 1.

Preparation

1. Cut a circle, square, triangle, and rectangle out of lightweight cardboard or construction paper. The shapes should be proportionate to the shapes in the drawings on the next page.
2. Create a poster using the words, "Stress is the way I respond to events in my life."
3. Make enough copies of "Life Events" for each person.
4. Have "Stress Management Worksheets" prepared for "Ways of Managing Stress," in Part 2.

POSSIBLE SCHEDULE (1 DAY)

8:30 Arrive, get acquainted
9:00 Play the Stress Game
9:30 Define Stress and Explore Stress Levels
10:30 Break (provide light snack)
11:00 Stress Thermometer
12:00 Lunch (A 6-foot submarine sandwich would be fun)
1:00 Games or group building exercises
1:30 Relaxation Exercise
3:00 Break
3:15 Ways of Managing Stress
4:00 Drama; Reflections
4:45 Closing Worship
5:15 Clean up and departure

Part One: Stress—What and When?

Play a Game

Ask for six volunteers. Divide them into three pairs. Each pair is to choose one person to be an instructor and the other to be a designer.

Follow these directions with one pair at a time: Give the designer the geometric shapes you cut out before the program. Give the instructor a copy of one of the drawings on this page. The instructor is to describe the drawing in such a way that the designer can create an exact replica using the geometric shapes. Explain that the pair creating a replica in the shortest amount of time will win.

The rest of the group is to cheer the first pair, boo the second pair, and pressure the third pair.

When all three pairs have finished, bring the youth together for discussion. Ask: How did it feel to be cheered? booed? pressured? Did the reactions of the group affect your performance? Introduce the purpose of this session: to define stress and to identify some of its causes.

Drawing One   Drawing Two   Drawing Three

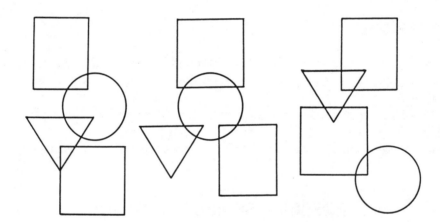

Define Stress

Write "Stress" in large letters on a chalkboard or a large sheet of paper. Ask youth to say the first thing that comes to mind when they hear the word stress. Write down their responses.

Display the poster that says, "Stress Is the Way I Respond to Events in My Life." Explain that different kinds of events, both pleasant and unpleasant, can result in stress. However, events do not cause stress, we cause stress by the way we react.

Explore Stress Levels

Give each person a copy of the "Life Event" worksheet (an application of "The Social Readjustment Rating Scale," by T. H. Holmes and R. H. Rahe in *Childstress! Understanding and Answering Stress Signals of Infants, Children, and Teenagers*, by Mary Susan Miller; Doubleday and Company, 1982; pages 22-23. Included in the original scale were three entries not applicable to children or youth). Ask persons to circle the events that apply to them. When they have finished, ask them to total their scores. Explain that the scores may be interpreted as follows:

Moderate Stress: 150-199
Medium Stress: 200-299
Severe Stress: over 300

Divide the youth into groups of three. Ask the groups to discuss the following:

● How do you feel about your level of stress?
● Do you think your level of stress is normal?
● What would you say to a best friend who received your score?

LIFE EVENT	VALUE
1. Death of a parent	100
2. Divorce of parents	73
3. Separation of parents	65
4. Parent's jail term	63
5. Death of a close family member (i.e., grandparent)	63
6. Personal injury or illness	53
7. Parent's remarriage	50
8. Suspension or expulsion from school	47
9. Parents' reconciliation	45
10. Long vacation (Christmas, summer, etc.)	45
11. Parent or sibling sickness	44
12. Mother's pregnancy	40
13. Anxiety over sex	39
14. Birth of new baby (or adoption)	39
15. New school or new classroom or new teacher	39
16. Money problems at home	38
17. Death (or moving away) of close friend	37
18. Change in studies	36
19. More quarrels with parents (or parents quarreling more)	35
20. Change in school responsibilities	29
21. Sibling going away to school	29
22. Family arguments with grandparents	29
23. Winning school or community awards	28

24. Mother going to work or stopping work   26

25. School beginning or ending   26

26. Family's living standard changing   25

27. Changing in personal habits—i.e., bedtime, homework, etc.   24

28. Trouble with parents—lack of communication, hostility   23

29. Change in school hours, schedule, or courses   20

30. Family's moving   20

31. A new school   20

32. New sports, hobbies, family recreation activities   19

33. Change in church activities—more involved or less   19

34. Change in social activities—new friends, loss of old ones, peer pressure   18

35. Change in sleeping habits—staying up later, giving up nap, etc.   16

36. Change in number of family get-togethers   15

37. Change in eating habits—going on or off diet, new way of family
    cooking   15

38. Vacation   13

39. Christmas   12

40. Breaking home, school or community rules   11

Stress Thermometer

Ask persons to imagine there is a thermometer lying on the floor across the center of the room. On one wall post a sign that says Freezing and on the opposite wall a sign that says Boiling. Read the following situations. Ask group members to stand at the spot on the thermometer that best represents the amount of stress each situation would create for them. Encourage the youth to express feelings about the situations.

1. You have been dating the same person for almost a year. Today, after a terrible argument, you break up.
2. Your mother is waiting for you when you get home from school. She tells you that your family will move to a new community next month.
3. You are trying to do your homework during study hall so that you can to go work after school. Today, the room is especially noisy.
4. You feel you are being manipulated by your best friend.
5. The bell rings just as you get to the last question on a final exam.
6. Your brother or sister has taken your favorite compact disc and won't give it back.
7. Even though you have a date, you father orders you to stay home tonight.
8. Your parents refuse to give you guidelines to follow as you make a major decision.
9. You are left alone for a week.

Gather the group together. Invite the youth to complete the following sentences:

1. To me, stress is _____ .

2. One thing I have learned is _____ .

3. Right now, I feel _____ .

Part Two: Stress—How Can I Live with It?

Relaxation Exercise

During this activity, persons will physically tighten different muscle groups in their bodies and then relax them. Invite youth to sit or to lie down so that they are comfortable and cannot touch anyone else. Ask them to take two or three deep breaths and to concentrate on the sound of your voice. Then invite them to tighten the following muscle groups, in the order suggested; to keep them tense for a count of five; and then to relax them. Youth should tighten the muscles of their

1. feet and toes
2. legs
3. buttocks
4. stomach
5. chest
6. hands and arms
7. face and neck

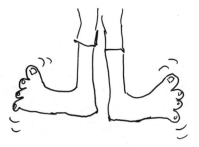

When the youth have finished the exercise, ask them to gather in a circle and to discuss their feelings about the experience.

Images of Stress Management

Explain the purpose of Part Two, telling the youth that they will be exploring ways of coping with stress, not eliminating it. Ask a volunteer to let you borrow any item from his or her pocket or purse. Ask: In what way is this item like managing stress effectively? How is it different? Record answers on a chalkboard or a large sheet of paper. Ask: What item in your favorite room in your house is most like managing stress effectively? Again, record responses.

Ways of Managing Stress

Divide the youth into four groups. Ask each group to complete a "Stress Management Worksheet." Each group should choose a different "Source of Help" from among the following: self, friends, adults, God.

Stress Management Worksheet

Source of Help: _____ .

1. Complete the following statement: Wouldn't it be nice if our source of help _____

_____ .

2. List twelve activities that are specific ways of using your source of help to manage stress. (For example, you can help yourself by doing a relaxation activity or by exercising.)

a. _____ .

b. _____ .

c. _____ .

d. _____ .

e. _____ .

f. _____ .

g. _____ .

h. _____ .

i. _____ .

j. _____ .

k. _____ .

l. _____ .

3. Review your list. Place a star by the items that seem most important.
4. Choose one of the starred items. List three advantages of this activity, two ways you can get started with it, and one way you can continue with it.

Advantages:

_____

_____

_____ .

Getting Started:

_____

_____

_____ .

Continuing:

_____

_____

_____ .

When all the groups have completed the worksheet, bring them together to report. Invite the groups to report their sources of help and the items they starred. Record their responses on a chalkboard or a large sheet of paper. Ask the groups to summarize the information they listed in number 4.

Dramas

Ask volunteers to do roleplays using what they have learned about managing stress. They are to roleplay either the situations from "Stress Thermometer," in part 1, or the following:

1. You are the center of a conversation that also includes your parent(s), two friends, and a trusted adult. You sister has been doing drugs for about six months, and her behavior is tearing you apart. Talk about your feelings; ask each of the people around you for help.

2. You were chosen to play an instrumental solo at the school concert tonight. You practiced well and know your part. This afternoon you begin to feel sick to your stomach. Now, as the concert approaches, you feel more and more jittery. You are in your room getting dressed. A parent calls you to dinner. Who will you ask for help? yourself? a parent? adult? God?

3. In seventeen days, you will graduate from high school. You feel as if you have been waiting for this event all your life. You are too excited for words. Lately you have had trouble concentrating in school, and you have been getting angry easily. Sometimes, you feel like running away. How do you handle this stress?

After each roleplay, ask: How do you feel about the way stress was managed in this situation? Which of the helps we chose earlier were used? What would you have done the same way? What would you have done differently?

Reflection

Explain that some people keep a journal as a way of responding to stress. Give the youth pencils and paper, and ask them to imagine that they are writing in their personal journals. Ask them to write about the pressures in their lives and the ways they believe they can effectively cope with stress.

✝   Closing Worship   ✝

In preparation for worship, invite group members to prepare statements about stressful situations in their lives. The statements should begin with the word *when*. For example, "When I can't answer the questions on a test, . . ."

Begin worship by inviting volunteers to read **Psalm 23:1-4; Psalm 46;1-2;** and **Revelation 21:6.** Allow time for silent reflection at the end of each reading.

Ask the group to sing "Spirit of the Living God."

Ask youth to read aloud their statements about stressful situations in their lives. After each has been read, the group is to say, "God is with you always."

Invite the youth to gather in a circle and hold hands. Invite volunteers to say sentence prayers expressing their feelings about this event. After all the prayers have been offered, ask the youth to say the Lord's Prayer together.

—Larry F. Beman

5

EASTER EVERY DAY

PURPOSE: *To help youth understand that they can live and celebrate the Easter victory throughout the year.*

Preparation

Choose a spring weekend for the retreat. Plan the retreat to last from twenty-four to forty-eight hours, beginning with dinner on Friday evening. Choose a comfortable setting such as a camp, a retreat center, a mountain or lakeside cabin, or a youth room or fellowship hall. The setting should be informal and flexible and provide areas for cooking and group activities, for group discussion and worship, and for outdoor exploration and activities.

This chapter will suggest a number of activities for the retreat. Choose the ones that are most meaningful for your group. Form a planning committee that will decide on a working schedule. Share the committee's planning with all group members before the retreat.

POSSIBLE SCHEDULE (3 day)

FRIDAY
    6:00 Arrive at retreat location
    7:00 Lenten meal
    8:00 Lenten activities
   10:00 Worship

SATURDAY
    8:00 Easter breakfast
    9:00 Easter activities
   11:00 Free time
   12:00 Lunch
    1:00 Recreation and free time
    4:00 Easter Bible study
    5:30 Dinner
    7:00 New Life Party (movie, dance, or
           games)
   10:00 Worship

SUNDAY
    6:30 Sunrise worship service
    8:00 Breakfast
    9:00 Planning to be Easter people
   11:00 Closing and clean-up
   12:00 Lunch
    3:00 Return to church

Easter is the celebration of celebrations, the most joyful observance of the Christian year. It is the victorious remembrance of Christ's resurrection and final victory over every power of death and evil. The Easter season begins on Easter Sunday and lasts for fifty days, in remembrance of the days the resurrected Christ remained on the earth before his ascension into heaven. During those fifty days, Christ appeared to the disciples and to others, amazing them and demonstrating his power and new life to them. Youth can carry out the retreat theme, "Easter Every Day," in every part of the retreat experience. The time schedule, the meals, the snacks, the music, the worship, the group activities, can all contribute to the joyful mood of the event.

Begin the retreat with a Lenten meal, such as a pancake supper or an agape meal (see pp. 41-42). Food should be simple, but adequate for hungry youth. For table decorations, use purple candles, wooden crosses, crowns of thorns, pieces of silver, or other Lenten symbols. Consider using the money you save by this simple menu as a special offering to a mission cause, and place that amount in a basket in a visible place.

Choose Lenten activities that meet the needs and interests of your group. A list of activities follows.

Close the evening with a simple Tenebrae service in remembrance of the crucifixion of Jesus. Light a number of candles on a table. Ask one group member to read the story of the Crucifixion from **Mark 15:1-38.** Ask another group member to extinguish candles as the story is read, gradually darkening the worship area. Candles could be extinguished after verses 5, 15, 17, 19, 20, 24, 32, and 37. Verses 38 and 39 should be read in complete darkness. The reader can use a small flashlight. The group members should leave the worship area in silence.

Begin Saturday with an Easter breakfast. The food should be festive and abundant (see suggestions at the end of this program). Choose Easter activities that will meet the needs and interests of youth. A list of possible activities follows. For the Easter New Life Party, choose activities that your group members enjoy, such as a movie, a dance, fellowship games, a bonfire, or a talent show.

Celebrate new life in the closing worship for the evening. Use colorful butterflies as a symbol of new life in Christ. Describe the process that a caterpillar undergoes in order to become a butterfly. Perhaps you can find a children's story with illustrations to assist you in presenting the story. Read **2 Corinthians 5:16-17.** Invite the group members to think about areas of their own life that need the new life Christ offers.

Continue the celebration of new life on Sunday morning with a sunrise service. Watch the sun rise together, then read the story of the resurrection of Jesus, **Matthew 28:1-20.** Light Easter candles to welcome the resurrected Christ.

After breakfast, have a concluding session focusing on the future. Reread the concluding words of Matthew's Gospel, **Matthew 28:16-18.** As a group, ask yourselves these questions:

- What are some places in our community that need new life?
- How can we as Easter people show our faith in our community?
- What can we do to bring new joy and new life to our church?
- What mission projects do we want to do in the coming months as we continue to be Easter people every day?

Lenten Activities

Make crosses. According to legend, the dogwood tree was once tall and straight and strong. Then it was used to make the cross Jesus died on. The dogwood tree was so ashamed that it would not be comforted. Christ comforted the tree by changing its shape. It was no longer tall and straight and strong. It became thin and twisted, so that a cross never again could be made from it. The blossom of the tree became an annual reminder of the death of Jesus. Its blossom is in the shape of a cross, with a crown of thorns in the center and nail prints on each petal. Make simple crosses from dogwood or other branches by lashing two sticks together. Decorate the retreat setting with the crosses.

Discuss difficult situations. Think about situations in the world or community that need new life. Using magazines and newspapers, make a collage of pictures that show brokenness, death, and sadness. Discuss this question: How does the symbol of the cross help us when we face difficult situations?

Respond to case studies. Choose several of the following case studies for group discussion. Consider these questions in relation to the case studies:

- What are your feelings as you imagine this incident?
- What might you do to cope with your fears and feelings?
- How might you help the persons who are directly involved?

Case Study 1: Your friend's father dies of a heart attack. Just last weekend you saw him playing golf.

Case Study 2: A classmate is killed in a car crash. The driver of the car that hit your friend's car is drunk.

Case Study 3: An older woman in your church dies. The youth group visited with her and caroled to her at Christmas. Recently the church gave her a party on her ninetieth birthday.

Read John 14:1-3. Rewrite this passage in your own words.

Write epitaphs. Ask group members to imagine that their life has ended. They have attained their goals and their life has been fulfilled. Distribute pencils and paper and ask each group member to write his or her own epitaph.

Make a banner. Provide burlap, felt, and fabric glue. Make Lenten banners, using the symbols of Jesus' crucifixion. The symbols might include a crown of thorns, a whip, a money bag, a cross, a crowing cock, palm branches, a basin and towel, and other symbols you may think of.

Easter Activities

Share an incident from a story.
My father (and I) once looked at a bird lying on its side against the curb near our house.
"Is it dead, Papa?" I was six and could not bring myself to look at it.
"Yes," I heard him say in a sad and distant way.
"Why did it die?"
"Everything that lives must die."
"Everything?"
"Yes."
"You too Papa? And Mama?"
"Yes."
"And me?"
"Yes," he said. Then he added in Yiddish, "But may it be only after you live a long and good life, my Asher."
I couldn't grasp it. I forced myself to look at the bird. Everything alive would one day be as still as that bird?
"Why?" I asked.
"That's the way [God] made the world, Asher."
"Why?"
"So life would be precious, Asher. Something that is yours forever is never precious."
—From *My Name Is Asher Lev* by Chaim Potok

Have a scavenger hunt for signs of death and life. Ask group members to choose an individual area to explore. Ask them to look for signs of death and signs of life. Signs of death might be broken sticks, old trash, dead leaves. Signs of life might be flowers, green grass, insects, moss on a hollow log. Regroup and display the signs.

Conduct Bible interviews. Assign group members biblical characters who were present at the Crucifixion or at the empty tomb (Mary Magdalene, Peter, Joanna, Mary the mother of Jesus, the soldiers, the chief priests, Joseph of Arimathea, people in the crowd, Barabbas, Nicodemus). Use a concordance to help you research the parts each character played in the story of the Crucifixion and Easter morning. After completing the research, ask one group member to serve as a reporter who interviews the witnesses to all these happenings. The reporter can ask questions such as the following:

● What did you see?
● What did you hear?
● What did you do?
● What does it mean?

Write poems about how Easter affects our life. Help the group members write simple poems using one of these two patterns. Samples are provided.

first line	one word	Service
second line	two words, describing first word	Sunrise worship
third line	three words, describing first word	Pancake breakfast fundraiser
fourth line	four word clause about first word	Honoring God, helping others
fifth line	word used in line one, or a synonym of it	Celebration

40

first line	one word	Jesus
second line	two words, verb and adverb	died recently
third line	three words, adjectives	wrapped, anointed, entombed
fourth line	four words, a phrase	leaving his disciples alone—
fifth line	five word sentence	Jesus rose from the dead!

Share the Easter poems with one another and use them later in a worship service in your church or print them in your church newsletter or worship bulletin.

Study the post-resurrection appearances of Jesus: **Matthew 28:8-10, 16-20; Luke 24:13-48; John 20:10-18, 19-23, 24-29; 21:1-14, 15-23.** Discuss these questions after studying the Scriptures:

● How are these accounts similar? How are they different?
● The people to whom Jesus appeared were all surprised. How did they show their surprise? What did they do?
● When their initial surprise was over, what did they do?
● What did Jesus say in these appearances?
● What message do these stories have for us today?

Easter Eating

For retreat meals and snacks, choose foods that reinforce the theme Easter Every Day. The following recipes present some possibilities. Look in cookbooks and Easter books for others.

Passover Salad is a reminder of the slavery in Egypt that God ended in the Exodus. The apples and other ingredients remind us of the mortar the slaves mixed. The sweet taste of the salad reminds us that slavery is ended.

6 medium apples, grated or finely chopped
½ cup raisins
½ cup chopped nuts
1 teaspoon brown sugar
¼ cup sour cream

Mix and serve.

Pretzels. Christians in the Roman Empire made simple bread of flour, salt, and water and shaped it in the form of arms crossed in prayer. Pretzels are a traditional Lenten food.

1 package yeast
1¼ cup warm water
1 tablespoon sugar
¼ cup melted margarine or butter
¼ cup wheat germ
3¾ cups flour
1 egg
coarse salt

Dissolve yeast in water. Add the next five ingredients in the order given. Knead the dough until smooth, adding flour as necessary. Roll the dough between the hands to form long, pencil-thin rope. Put lightly beaten egg in a shallow bowl. Put coarse salt in another bowl. Take 8-inch lengths of dough. Holding the ends, dip one side of the lengths first into the egg and then lightly into the salt. Place on a heavily greased cookie sheet with the salt side up. Bend into little arms, crosses, and other shapes symbolic of Lent. Bake at 425 degrees until well-browned.

Pancakes. Pancakes are a traditional Lenten food. On the night before Ash Wednesday (the beginning of Lent), families used the flour in their cupboards to make pancakes rather than gathering food that would remain unused during the Lenten fast.

Fish. A meal of fish reminds us of the meal Jesus prepared for the disciples after they had fished all night and caught nothing (**John 21:1-14**).

Agape meal. A simple meal of bread, cheese, fruit, and water reminds us of the simple meals the disciples and the early followers of the risen Christ shared. The Lord's Supper was celebrated often in the early church at the conclusion of such a meal.

Hot Cross Buns. This sweet roll with its cross of frosting is traditionally eaten during Lent.

2 packages active dry yeast
⅓ cup water
⅓ cup milk, scalded
½ cup salad oil or melted shortening
⅓ cup sugar
¾ teaspoon salt
3½ to 4 cups sifted flour
½ to 1 teaspoon cinnamon
3 eggs
⅔ cup currants or raisins
1 slightly beaten egg white
sifted confectioner's sugar

Soften yeast in warm water. Combine milk, salad oil, sugar, and salt. Cool to lukewarm. Sift together 1 cup flour and cinnamon; stir into milk mixture. Add eggs; beat well. Stir in yeast and currants or raisins. Add remaining flour to make a soft dough. Cover with a damp cloth. Let rise in a warm place until double (about 1 1/2 hours). Punch down. Roll or pat out to 1/2 inch thickness on lightly floured surface. Cut in rounds with 2 1/2 inch biscuit cutter. Place on greased baking sheet about 1 1/2 inches apart. Cover and let rise until almost double (about 1 hour). Cut shallow cross in each bun with scissors. Brush tops with egg white. Bake in moderate oven (350 or 375 degrees) 12 to 15 minutes or until done. Add confectioner's sugar to remaining egg white. Use this frosting to make crosses on warm buns. Makes about 2 dozen.

Stone Soup. A hungry traveler needed some soup. No one had the ingredients to spare. The traveler placed a stone in a pot. "I have a stone," he said. "What can you add?" One by one, the villagers found a carrot, a potato, a small piece of meat, and a tomato to add to the stone. Make stone soup by providing broth and asking each group member to bring one ingredient. Or provide all the ingredients, and ask each group member to prepare the ingredient and add it to the soup pot at the appropriate time. Making this soup demonstrates the unity of Easter people.

Unleavened bread or pita bread. This bread reminds us of the Last Supper. The disciples would have eaten unleavened bread at their meals.

✝   Closing Worship   ✝

For the closing service, you will need a daffodil bulb and a daffodil (in bloom) for everyone. Give each person a bulb and place the blooming daffodils in the center of the circle or on the altar.

With each person holding his or her bulb, have someone read **Matthew 27:45-56.** Sing "Were You There" or some other appropriate Good Friday hymn. In silence, or having persons share their thoughts, ask the group to reflect on:

● The feelings of the women at the crucifixion.
● The bulb in their hands. What does it look like, feel like? Does it look alive or dead? Ask: If you saw the bulb just lying on the sidewalk, would you think that it had any possibility for beauty or new life?
● How is the daffodil bulb like our lives? Like a person facing failure or death without hope?

Read **Matthew 28:1-10.**
Sing "Morning Has Broken." As the group sings the song, have each youth go to the center or altar and get a blooming daffodil, replacing it with the bulb.

Talk about when and where youth have discovered new life in their own lives. Pray prayers of thanksgiving for new life.

Celebrate Holy Communion and conclude by singing "Christ the Lord Is Risen Today."

—Hope Ward

6

GET BEHIND ME, SATAN

PURPOSE: *To help youth become more aware of the dangers of satanic worship.*

Consider the following grim news story that occurred on April 12, 1989, in Matamoros, Mexico, just south of the U.S. border:

"A satanic cult of drug smugglers who sacrificed and apparently cannibalized humans slaughtered 12 people (the total later rose to 15), including a U.S. college student on spring break . . . 21-year old University of Texas student Mark Kilroy.

" . . . Kilroy apparently was chosen at random by drug smugglers who had hoped human sacrifices would protect them from harm. Cult members 'were told to pick one Anglo male that particular night,' " (Sheriff's Lt. George) Gavito said.

"The cult had been involved in human sacrifices for about nine months," he said, "and prayed to the devil 'so the police would not arrest them, so bullets would not kill them and so they could make more money.' "

"Authorities found candles and kettles full of body parts and animal bones," said Oran Neck, chief U.S. Customs agent in Brownsville." (From an Associated Press story reported in *The Quincy Herald*, April 12, 1989.)

Even though the vast majority of youth never participate in devil worship, nearly all youth are exposed to it through television, movies, and some heavy metal music. This event will help youth increase their awareness of satanism, sort through their feelings in response to it, and become more aware of the resources in Christian faith which help them deal with all forms of evil.

Preparation

As you plan this event, consider three suggestions. Since this subject can arouse strong feelings, have at least one staff person along who is a trained counselor. Second, let the youth play an important part in planning the event. Youth know what questions they have, what resource people they may have heard at school, and how much time they are willing to spend on this difficult subject. Third, remember throughout that learning about satanism will not defeat God. Rather, our own faith will be stronger and we will be better prepared to deal with satanic cults if we should encounter one. Let Christian hope permeate the entire event!

Some planning options include:

Ask a police officer or other person in your community who has some firsthand knowledge or training about satanism to make Friday night's presentation.

Ask the pastor to plan for communion on Friday evening.

Study the subject of satanism at the library. Check out numerous articles and books for the retreat. (See the bibliography at the end of this event for suggestions)

Check out and preview denominational videos and films on the occult. Borrow and triple-check the working condition of all audio-visual aids!

Secure several balloons and a helium tank for the closing worship.

POSSIBLE SCHEDULE (3 Day)

FRIDAY

    6:00 Session 1: Satanism, black masses, and the facts
    8:00 Informational movie or group games
    9:00 Worship 1: Communion: Drawing near to the right one

SATURDAY

    8:00 Breakfast
    9:00 Active games, including tug-of-war and leapfrog
  10:00 Session 2: Evil and the divine/human tug-of-war
  11:00 Small group discussion or learning centers
  12:00 Lunch
    1:00 Free time for personal reading, individual reflection, rest
    2:00 Learning centers: What makes the pump handle look tasty?
    4:00 Group recreational time
    5:00 Supper
    6:00 Movies for entertainment (or films about satanism)
    9:30 Worship 2: All the right moves

SUNDAY

    8:00 Breakfast
    9:00 Session 3: Putting on the armor of God
  11:00 Closing worship: Celebration of God's victory
  12:00 Lunch, pack, and leave for home

SESSION 1: Satanism, black masses, and the facts

Open session 1 with a presentation by a police officer or other person who has had contact with satanism. Ask him or her to describe the main beliefs and practices of satanists, and to explain several of the most common satanic symbols. Ask him or her to talk about the actual extent of devil worship in your area, the profile of those most likely to be involved in such cult activities, what law enforcement officers can do to combat devil worship (with its associated criminal activity), and what churches and average citizens can do about the problem.

When the speaker has finished, ask her or him to remain for the rest of the evening as a resource person. Ask the youth to get into groups of three or four. Using the speaker's presentation (plus any other resources you provide), have each small group gather information about one particular topic, such as the following:

- a chart contrasting Christian beliefs with satanist beliefs
- a description of unusual satanic rituals or behaviors (with definitions) such as the black mass, banding, and communicating in strange codes
- drawings and explanations of satanic symbols

- a list of warning signs which indicate that someone might be involved in devil worship
- a list of possible reasons devil worship or the occult might appeal to some youth
- short descriptions of biblical passages which involve the devil
- a list of noteworthy or bizarre satanist-related crimes from news accounts.

Note: many of the preceding lists will require advance research by the group leader, so the youth will have the required information readily available.

Have a representative from each small group tell the group's information to all the groups. If there is not enough time, simply post the written work of each group and allow time for final questions or comments.

WORSHIP: Drawing near to the right one

Open this communion service with one or more familiar songs. Then read **James 4:7-8** to the group. Comment on the passages stressing that drawing near to God is one way to resist the devil (as well as all other forms of evil and wrongdoing). Note that participating in Holy Communion is one way to draw near to God. Say that one reason this retreat includes several worship services is that worship is one important resource for resisting evil.

Read **Luke 24:13-35**. Since this is a long passage, you may choose to divide the reading into three or four parts, asking one youth to read each part. After the reading, express the hope that, just as Jesus' disciples recognized him when the bread was broken, our eyes might also be opened in a special way to him in the breaking of bread and that we might draw closer to him during this retreat. If possible, use a whole loaf of bread so that it can be broken in the presence of the youth.

SESSION 2: Evil and the divine/human tug-of-war

Before the session, have a tug-of-war contest which pits the leaders against the youth. Then play leapfrog as a group, with leaders and youth working together to reach a destination as quickly as possible.

46

Give each youth a Bible, a sheet of paper, a pencil and a copy of the following questions. Ask youth to answer the questions on the sheet of paper.

1. Carefully read **Luke 4:1-13**.
   ● In your opinion, does the devil exist?
   ● If you think so, then do you think the devil is responsible for all evil?
   ● If you do not think so, what does make us feel tempted to do evil?

2. Based upon **Luke 4** and your own best guess:
   ● What would the devil's goals be on earth?
   ● What powers does the devil have that ordinary humans do not have?

3. Rather than joining the devil's team, like playing leapfrog, Jesus engaged in a tug-of-war match against Satan's temptations, and won.
   ● What resources did Jesus use to win?
   ● Are those same resources available to us when we choose to resist evil?
   ● If humans play leapfrog with the devil (cooperate with or even worship him), what extra power or help does this give the devil toward meeting his earthly goals?

4. Carefully read **Romans 7:14-25**.
   ● Does this describe leapfrog or tug-of-war?
   ● Who is on the other team, in Paul's view?

5. Reread **Romans 7:14-25**, underlining or noting the parts which especially describe you.
   ● Why is it that Christians, who should be attracted to doing good, can also be tempted to do evil?
   ● Does being tempted to do evil automatically put one in the power of evil?
   ● What answers to the problem of temptation does Paul give us?

6. Read **Romans 8:31-39**. Since Paul wrote **Romans 8:31-39** as well as **Romans 7:14-25**, how do you think they fit together? For instance:
   ● How does the victory in **Romans 8** solve the problem of **Romans 7**?
7. Think about your relationship with Jesus.
   ● In what ways do you play tug-of-war with Jesus, and in what ways do you play leapfrog?
   ● If you cooperated with Jesus in every way, how much more powerful could he become in your life? in the world?
8. What would you have to do, specifically, to enable Jesus to help you resist the temptation Paul describes in **Romans 7** and to grow toward the kind of faith Paul expresses in **Romans 8**?

At this point, consider two options. One is to have youth discuss their answers in small groups to finish out the session. You may wish to end with a devotional or other worship experience. An alternative is to make the preceding private reflection one station (or divide into two) among the following learning centers, thereby combining the two activities.

Learning Centers:
What Makes the Pump Handle Look Tasty?

Learning centers are separate, simultaneously-offered educational stations (such as a table covered with newspaper articles, a filmstrip in a dark corner, and so on), which explore various angles of a single topic. Individuals can be completely free during learning center time, or learning centers can be designed so that small groups stay together as they move from place to place. Decide in advance whether time limits will be imposed and whether youth will visit all stations or only those that interest them. Each station should have simple, written instructions, and all the supplies needed. Learning centers are limited only by your imagination, but do use a variety of methods and media. Here are several ideas for learning centers:

1. To illustrate the lure of evil, secure a copy of Garrison Keillor's *Lake Wobegon Days*, so youth can read the story about the pump handle on pages 306-307. You may choose to secure the audiotape of Keillor reading this story. Have a tape recorder available so youth can listen to the audiotape. Ask the youth to respond to these questions:

   ● What is the source of temptation?
   ● Does evil have the power to lure us toward it? Why or why not?

   Discuss the power that evil has on peer pressure to do wrong and on the role of friends in helping us to avoid sin.
2. One lure of satanism is the desire to have power or control. Ask youth to think or talk about areas in their lives where they have some real power or control. These might include choices about how much to study, the way we take care of our bodies, the influence we have on others. Have available paper and envelopes, along with the addresses of legislators. Invite youth to write letters about issues that concern them, so the youth can exercise some political power on the spot. Reinforce their feelings of power by providing an article about the economic clout of teenagers.
3. With an adult leader, let youth roleplay tough situations (use a video camera if possible) such as being pressured into playing ouija, witnessing to a satanist who mocks the youth's cross necklace, dating a satanist, or dealing with a friend who is fascinated by satanic songs about suicide.

4. Tape a large sheet of butcher paper to a wall. On the paper list groups to which youth belong (such as family, friends, church, town, school, country, youth group, choir). Give each youth a crayon or felt-tipped marker and ask him or her to sign under each group where he or she is a member. Ask them to make two lists: things groups do for them, and things they can do for those groups.

FAMILY	CHURCH	SCHOOL	CHOIR	PEP BAND
Martha *Ramon*	*Peggy*	*Juanita*	*Martha*	*Ramon*

5. One lure of satanism is often hopelessness. Have one center that focuses on grace and salvation. Ask the pastor or some other adult who is knowledgeable and communicates well with youth to explain briefly what grace is and how it works in the Christian life. A good explanation of grace is found on pages 48-54 in *Faithful Members: The Doctrines and Duties of the Christian Faith* (Graded Press, 1988). Invite youth to think of ways the lives of the satanists mentioned in the news story at the beginning of this event could have been different if they had known about God's grace.

6. To illustrate the goodness of Christian salvation by using contrast, have a station where youth "reverse paraphrase" **Psalm 23** (put the opposite meaning in their own words, such as "the devil watches over me, and so I'll forever be starving"). Compare the reverse paraphrase with the Psalm itself. Try this technique with other passages.

7. Use the following warning signs of satanic obsession as a basis for discussion about how to deal with a friend who draws pentagrams on his or her school books, about whether it is safe to assume that people who listen to heavy metal music are actually satanists, and about why youth think satanists might dwell on themes of murder and suicide:
   a. Preoccupation with death, devil worship, suicide, and the afterworld.
   b. Abrupt emotional change in attitude, including rebellious and violent behavior.
   c. Unusual interest in books on the occult and roleplaying and fantasy games.
   d. Obsession with heavy-metal rock music with lyrics promoting murder, suicide, and sadistic behavior.
   e. Dressing in all black clothing and wearing jewelry such as upsidedown crosses, pentagrams, and anarchy symbols. (Anarchy symbols are any symbols of anarchic groups or satanic cults. They include the clenched fist with the first and fourth fingers making horns, the swastika, a clenched fist, and so on.)
   f. Drawing satanic symbols on the back of hands or on books and papers.
   g. Continuous writing, talking or communicating backward in a code or unfamiliar alphabet.

Worship:All the Right Moves

The focus of this worship service is God's gift of freedom and the responsibility that accompanies that gift. After opening songs, help the youth recall their right moves. Read the following Scriptures to the youth: **Psalm 51:1-7, 10, Isaiah 1:18, John 8:7-11.** Give each youth a sheet of paper and a pencil and ask him or her to write a thank-you note to God for freedom, belonging, and salvation. Ask some youth to read their thank you notes aloud as an act of praise. To tie this service into the morning session, perhaps one of the youth or adults could offer a meditation about cooperation with God called "Leapfrogging with God." It could be based on Romans 7 and 8, and the strength that comes in realizing that "Nothing can separate us from the love of Christ." Conclude with songs which express a sense of belonging to the group and to Christ such as "We are One in the Spirit."or "Children of the Light" (from the *Youth Praise* tape.)

Session 3: Putting On the Armor of God

The purpose of this session is to help youth explore the resources of the Christian faith in resisting satanism, evil, and temptation.

Reread one or more of the following temptation stories in **Matthew 4:1-11, Mark 1:12-13, Luke 4:1-13.** On a large sheet of paper or on a chalkboard list the temptations Jesus faced, and discuss some reasons why they might have been tempting for Jesus. Beside each temptation, write the way Jesus resisted it.

Next, ask the youth to carefully examine **Ephesians 6:10-18.** Note that the author is talking about spiritual powers of evil and the equipment a Christian has to defend himself or herself. List the various elements of the "whole armor of God" and ask the youth how each one could be a help against satanism. (Truth, for example, is a powerful weapon against one whom Scripture calls "the father of lies." **(John 8:44)** You may want to have a Bible dictionary to check the definitions of some of the words in this passage. Ask each youth to identify for himself or herself one element of Paul's "armor of God" that would be particularly helpful for him or her.

Say: "Individually, rewrite the temptation story, but substitute yourself for Jesus. List as many temptations as possible in your new temptation story, and feel free to apply Jesus' and/or Paul's answers to those temptations. Use more than one answer if it fits. Make the answers practical."

50

† Closing Worship †

Build this worship service around your group's list of resources in Christian faith for resisting satanism and other temptations. Before or during the service, have youth write out two lists on separate sheets of paper:

1. Things for which I need forgiveness
2. Things I will do, beginning today, to grow toward mental, physical, and spiritual wholeness.

Have them seal the second list in a self-addressed envelope and give it to you, with the understanding that you will mail it to them thirty days later. During the service, cut up the stack of confessions and put the pieces in balloons. Fill the balloons with helium and release them, pointing out "As high as the heavens are above the earth, so far has God removed our sins from us." Go around the circle, giving each youth a chance to lead worship for a moment. Have some youth read Scriptures which show the promises of the Gospel (hope, victory, encouragement and strength). Let others design and explain visual symbols of the parts of the armor of God (or cut them out from magazines). Have a youth paraphrase "A Mighty Fortress Is Our God." and let everyone sing the hymn. Give each youth a special momento with their name on it. Design the momento to remind them that they belong to the group and to Christ. These momentos may be such things as aluminum pocket crosses, handmade wooden crosses on thongs to wear around one's neck, or some symbolic reminder of the "whole armor of God." End with a lively, happy song of celebration.

Sources to consult:
Lake Wobegon Days by Garrison Keillor (Penguin Books, 1985).
The Screwtape Letters by C.S. Lewis (MacMillan Publishing Company, Inc., 1961).
"Flirting With the Devil" by Claudette McShane, *The Magazine for Christian Youth!*, May 1989.
People of the Lie: The Hope for Healing Human Evil by M. Scott Peck (Simon & Schuster, Inc., 1983).
The Satan Seller by Mike Warnke (Bridge Publishing Company, 1972).

—Jeffrey A. Rasche

7

SHOULD I WORK AFTER SCHOOL?

PURPOSE: *To help youth understand that the choices they make about when, how, and where they work, and how they spend their time and money, reflect the values they have in life.*

Preparation

Ahead of time, ask the following persons to conduct a panel discussion of "Teenage Employment: The Pros and Cons of After-School Jobs": a guidance counselor, an employer of teens, a youth counselor, a drug rehabilitation counselor, a church youth director from another church, and a high school principal. Send each panelist the list of questions included on the next page.

POSSIBLE SCHEDULE (2 days)

FRIDAY NIGHT
  7:00 Arrive, unpack, get settled
  7:30 Panel discussion
  8:30 Talk about why youth work
  9:00 Small groups
  9:30 Discuss schedules in larger group
10:00 Worship
10:30 Snacks and recreation
12:00 Lights out

SATURDAY
  8:00 Morning prayer
  8:30 Breakfast
  9:15 Group building and group games
10:30 Break
10:45 Browse through career choice options
      Discuss in small groups
      Plan the suggested skit
12:00 Lunch
  1:00 Group activity or game
  1:30 Each group presents skit
  2:00 Group discussion on choices and values
  2:45 Closing Worship
  3:00 Clean up and leave

Panel Discussion

Introduce the panelists and announce that the topic for discussion is "Teenage Employment: The Pros and Cons of After-School Jobs." Ask the panelists to discuss the following questions:

1. Do students who have traditional teenage jobs develop a greater sense of responsibility than those who do not?
2. Do students who have traditional teenage jobs gain more experience related to careers they will have as adults?
3. Do students who work in traditional teenage jobs appreciate a *good* job when they are in the work force?
4. Does having money they earned help teens spend the money wisely?
5. Does working fifteen or more hours per week interfere with school assignments?
6. Do students who work tend to miss more school?
7. Do working adolescents engage in fewer extracurricular activities than their nonworking peers?
8. As far as preparing students for careers, is volunteer work better than work in traditional teenage jobs?
9. Do students who work in paying jobs interact more with adults than students who do not work?
10. Is it necessary for some students to work to supplement their family financially?
11. Are the grades of students who work poorer than other students' grades?
12. Does having to work for money give adolescents a sense that their work is meaningful?
13. What about the long-term effects of after-school jobs?

- Will youth who do not work have an unrealistic attitude toward money that will keep them dependent on their parents too long?
- Will youth who work have grades too low for scholarships or too low for college entrance?
- Is the amount of money teens earn worth the possible tradeoff of poor grades?
- Does teen employment offer more contact with adults so that youth can learn good work habits they'll have for life?
- Do teens who work at minimum-wage jobs trade off long-term goals for short-term financial gain?

One segment of the teen population, farm youth, have always worked long hours after school and on weekends. If you live in a rural community, ask your panel to shift some of the questions to include the needs of farm youth.

After the panel discussion, say: "Some youth have a financial need to work after school. It may be necessary for some youth to supplement the family income. These youth may want to help the family financially by buying their own school clothes, food, or other necessities. Or they are working long hours because the income from their part-time job will be an important part of their college tuition. The accumulation of money or spending money only on themselves is not their top priority; and they are not buying the latest, most-expensive items on the market."

Explain to the group that those youth who work to supplement the family income may also develop a greater sense of responsibility than their nonworking peers. The youth who do hold jobs after school may not be able to participate in some extracurricular activities, but they are willing to make that sacrifice. Teens who work for this reason may achieve satisfaction knowing that they are contributing to the family and that there is a purpose for their work.

Say: "Some teens work part-time jobs so that they can buy the latest fashions, most-expensive clothes, stereos, and so on. These *in* things are the main temptations some working teens face. Many advertisements make teens want things they would never have cared about had they not been the *in* things to have." Explain to the youth that there are some parents who tell their teens that they may have the latest, most-expensive fads as long as the teens get jobs to pay for the luxuries. Most of these luxuries are priced higher than their actual value because they are targeted toward teens who have the money to spend. These teens are caught up in what has been termed *kidflation*. This is the inflation believed to be caused by those junior and senior high youth who have extra money to spend. Teens who want the latest styles and the latest fads, may never be satisfied, because there will always be something else to buy. Ask: When you think you have to have all the most-expensive brand names advertised, are you playing your game or someone else's?

Ask a youth to read **Ecclesiastes 5:10.** Have enough Bibles available so that the other youth may look at the Scripture as it is being read. Say: "When our first priority is the accumulation of money and the desire to buy things because they are the *in* things to have, we are neglecting our spiritual side. This desire may make us feel unhappy and unsatisfied. Because we are so caught up in spending money for all the *in* things, we may often feel that we do not have enough money to give to God and to the church."

Creating Schedules

Divide the group into three smaller groups and present each one with a scenario in which they must figure out schedules for a cheerleader, for a band member, and for a teen who must baby-sit his or her younger sibling. Youth are to allow time in the schedule for church activities, home chores, and homework as well. They are to decide whether the teens in the scenario have time for a part-time job. The following are the scenarios for the smaller groups:

```
┌─────────────────────────────────────┐
│         TUESDAY  Chelsea             │
│  8 a.m.     School                   │
│  Noon       Student Council mtg.     │
│  3 p.m.     Practice                 │
│  7 p.m.     Homework                 │
│  9:30 p.m.  Finish Homework          │
│             Sleep?                   │
└─────────────────────────────────────┘
```

GROUP 1—The Cheerleader

Chelsea is a cheerleader who practices on Tuesdays and Thursdays from 3:00 P.M. until 5:00 P.M. She must be at the weekly games from 6:00 P.M. until 10:00 P.M. on Fridays. Make a schedule for her that includes time for church activities, home chores, homework, and a part-time job if you decide she has enough time.

GROUP 2—The Band Member

Tammy is a band member who must practice on Monday, Wednesday, and Thursday from 3:15 P.M. until 5:15 P.M.. She must also play at the home games from 6:00 P.M. until 10:00 P.M. on Fridays. Make a schedule that includes home chores, homework, church activities, and a part-time job if you decide she has enough time.

GROUP 3—The Baby Sitter

Jason has to baby-sit his younger brother every day from 4:00 P.M. until 5:30 P.M., when his mother comes home from work. Plan a schedule that includes church activities, home chores, homework, and a part-time job if you decide he has enough time.

Worship

Review with the youth what they have talked about in this session. Ask them to remember all the pros and cons about working after school; and remind them that, when teens make a decision to work, they must also make other decisions. Say: "When you take a part-time job, you are setting priorities for yourself. Part of good stewardship involves planning your use of time to include church, home, and school responsibilities. Others may be looking to you for a Christian example of how to use time. If you are modeling creative uses of time, you can show others a way to live out their faith commitments in their own lives." Ask a youth to read the following prayer: "Dear Lord, we thank you for our talents and abilities. Help us to find ways to serve you and to be good stewards of our time and money. Help us to always put you first when choices must be made. Amen."

Career Choices

Ask a guidance counselor for pamphlets or other printed materials about career choices. Many schools have brochures explaining job descriptions, educational and other qualifications, future prospects, and so on for many different kinds of jobs. Also see how many magazine articles you can find about teens who work.

Say something like: "Take about twenty minutes to browse through the materials we have on career options. Choose one or two careers that really interest you. Later, we will talk about the effects of working after school on your career choices." As youth finish choosing, record their choices on the chalkboard or on a large sheet of paper. Divide the group into five groups for discussion of the effect of part-time jobs on future careers. (In a small-membership group, one person can represent a group. If you have a large group, you may want to have ten groups rather than five.) Give each group one of the following questions written on a three-by-five card and any magazine articles or other printed resources that relate to their question.

1. How might teens' working affect their career goals?
2. How might teens' working affect their health?
3. How might working help to develop a teen's sense of responsibility and self-worth?
4. How might working affect teens' getting scholarships or even attaining college admittance?
5. How might teens' working help them gain experience related to future careers?

Tell each group that they are to read the excerpts or articles. Ask youth to remember all the pros and cons of part-time jobs that were discussed in the previous session. Ask each group to think about their own career choices as they discuss the question assigned to their group. Youth who are working on the family farm or in the family business and who intend to continue working there as a career, will simply affirm their choice. Other youth who are working to help their family or to pay for college will have other feelings about working part-time. Still other youth will have ideas about how they want to improve their situations and not always work in relatively dead-end jobs. Ask each group to present a skit showing how teen jobs could affect their futures. Allow twenty to twenty-five minutes for group discussion and preparation. Encourage the use of humor to make serious points. Make yourself available if a group needs help, then ask the groups to perform their skits.

Ask for responses to the messages of the skits. What new ideas and feelings did people pick up from other groups?

Say something like: "The choices we make reflect our values. They say something about who we are and what is most important to us. Christian stewardship calls us to develop our talents and gifts as best we can. We need to remember the call of God as well as the financial demands and the pressure put on us by others when we make decisions about working while we are in school." Give each youth a pencil and a three-by-five card. Ask each youth to take a few minutes to think and then write, on one side of the card, some high values related to part-time jobs and careers.

Ask the youth to write, on the other side of the card, how working part-time will support their values. Ask youth to take their cards home and to put them where they can find them easily and can reflect on what they have written when they are thinking about values.

✝   Closing Worship   ✝

Read together the stanzas of "All Glory, Laud, and Honor." Close with the following prayer: "Dear Lord, let us give of our best to you because you gave of your best in Jesus Christ. We thank you for what you have done for us. May we help others come to you. Amen."

—Cynthia Stone

8

WHEN SOMEONE YOU LOVE DIES

PURPOSE: *To provide an opportunity for youth to explore the reality of death, as well as their feelings and reactions when someone they know dies.*

This event should provide an opportunity for youth to openly and honestly discuss their feelings about death, as well as what the Christian faith has to say about death.

Preparation

Because of the sensitive nature of the topic, advance preparation is crucial. Ahead of time make arrangements for the collage, the visit to the cemetery, the visit to the funeral home, and the funeral service. Also be sure you have all the supplies you need, including a casket box for each small group as well as pencils and paper for each youth.

The key to this weekend is the small group time. It is important to pick small group leaders who can deal with strong feelings. Adequately train the leaders before the retreat and make sure they understand the purpose of the weekend, how to facilitate small group sharing, and how not to shut off feelings that are expressed. The best way to train your small group leaders is to have them form a sharing group of their own and to have them work through the same curriculum that the youth will work through.

If possible have a professional counselor or psychologist speak to your leaders about normal grief and the coping mechanisms that the leaders may encounter in their groups.

> *I am the resurrection and the life. Those who believe in me, even though they die, will live, and everyone who lives and believes in me will never die.*
>
> —John 11:25

SUGGESTED SCHEDULE (3 days)

FRIDAY EVENING
   7:00 Arrive, unload, move in
   8:00 General Session
   9:00 Small Group No. 1
   10:00 Break
   10:30 Group Gathering and Worship

SATURDAY
   8:00 Breakfast
   8:30 General session
   9:00 Small Group No. 2
   10:30 Break
   11:00 Small Group No. 3
   12:30 Lunch
   1:00 Small Group No. 4
   2:30 Break
   3:00 Small group No. 5
   4:30 Break
   5:00 Dinner
   5:30 Group recreation/Free time
   7:00 Small Group No. 6
   8:30 Bonfire/Worship
   10:00 Free time/Games/Informal time

SUNDAY
   8:00 Breakfast
   8:30 General Session
   9:00 Trip to funeral home
   12:00 Noon lunch out
   1:00 Cradle with Care
   3:00 Closing Worship
   3:30 Pack and leave

Cemetery Visit

Allow time on the way to the retreat location for the group to visit a cemetery. When you arrive at the cemetery, have the group walk around in the cemetery and read the tombstones. Ask the youth to pay attention to their feelings as they do this activity. After ten to fifteen minutes, gather the group together to discuss the activity. If weather permits, have the discussion in the cemetery sitting among the tombstones. Ask the youth the following questions:

1. What did you feel as you walked through the cemetery?
2. What thoughts or memories were you aware of?
3. What are your fears, hopes, and expectations as we begin this retreat on death?

End the discussion by reminding the group about the weekend and its purpose.

General Session

After everyone has had time to unload and get moved in, bring the group together for an opening general session. Before the event, make a collage of newspaper articles and articles from other sources that involve death and post this collage of death on a wall. Collect at least two sources for every person present at the event. You may supplement the articles with words and phrases and with Scripture quotations.

Welcome everyone to the event by leading the group in singing a few rowdy, uplifting songs. Make whatever announcements and introductions are necessary. Finally, introduce the theme of the event, briefly go over the schedule, and give the group time to observe the collage of death. Tell the youth that they are to choose one article that means something to them. They will be sharing the article and their reaction to it at the first small group session.

After the youth have observed the collage of death, divide into groups of six to eight youth with an adult leader. Spread the groups out far enough so that each group has privacy.

Small Group No. 1: Death Is a Part of Life

Allow a few minutes for the group members to get to know each other. Have each person give their reaction to the visit to the cemetery. Ask the youth about some of the feelings, memories, fears, and thoughts that the visit raised.

Then ask each youth to tell which article he or she chose from the collage of death and why he or she chose it. Make a mental note of which youth have actually experienced the death of someone they have known. Ask the youth what experiences of death they have had.

Each small group is to have a small box for questions. Encourage the small group leaders to be creative in decorating the boxes like little caskets. Ask each youth to write one question he or she has about death or dying and to place it in the casket box. The questions are to be anonymous. To ensure that the questions are anonymous, tell each youth to write something and to put it in the box even if he or she doesn't have a question. If possible, allow enough time for the youth to write questions at the end of each session. Close with a prayer.

Free Time

The material to be covered during the weekend is extremely heavy and the schedule is tight. It is important that the breaks allow time for the youth to cut loose and let off tension. Depending on your group and how the weekend is going, you may want to shorten the small group sessions and lengthen the breaks. Some youth may prefer free time, while others may like more structured recreation. Go with what is best for your youth group. If you choose to have recreation, make sure that the games involve high activity levels.

Group Gathering

After the small group session and the break, bring the group back together for singing and games. Close with a worship service. After the worship, make sure that the sponsors are available to be with any of the youth who may have become upset because of the nature of the retreat and the issues they are dealing with in their own lives.

Saturday General Session

Begin with singing, games, and a morning devotion. If possible, have the general session outside, since the majority of the day will be spent in small group sessions.

Small Group No. 2: Dealing With Death

Have the group do a Scripture search with the following Bible passages. The youth are to read each passage and find out what the passage says on the topic of death.

Genesis 3:19	Psalm 23
Romans 8:35-39	Romans 12:15
Romans 14:7-9	John 11:17-35
John 11:25-26	1 Corinthians 12:12-13

Have each youth read his or her passage out loud and then report on what he or she thinks the passage says about the topic of death. Have the total group briefly discuss each passage and what they think it means.

Take a few minutes to have the group react to the Scriptures as a whole. You may use the following questions to guide the discussion:

● Is death natural?
● Why do we have to die?
● What does the Scripture say about us and our relationship with God as we face death?

Spend the rest of the time by answering questions from the casket box. Encourage youth to answer questions (not just the adult leader).

NOTE: If at any point in any session a youth becomes upset, you should give that youth precedence over the curriculum. If someone does become upset, encourage (but do not require) him or her to talk about what he or she is feeling. As the youth tells about his or her feelings, encourage others in the group to listen and, when appropriate, to show concern and to give support.

Use the last five minutes of the session for the youth to write a letter that talks about a time when someone they loved died. If a member has never experienced the loss of someone, they are to write about another kind of loss (someone moves away) or about what they think *might* happen if someone close to them died.

> Dear Jean,
>
> When I was 8 years old my Grandmother died. I thought she had just gone to the store and would soon return............

Small Group No. 3:
Sharing About a Time When We Lost Someone

Use the entire session to have the group members talk about their letters. If some of the youth have not finished their letters, you may use some of the time at the beginning of the

60

session to have them finish the letters. Ask for a volunteer to go first. The youth are to read the letters to the group. Then the small group leader is to ask them how they are feeling about what they wrote. Afterward, the entire group should have a chance to respond and to ask questions. If any youth has strong feelings about what he or she has written, it may take a long time. It is possible that the entire session may be spent dealing with one person and what he or she has written.

After each youth finishes, ask for another volunteer and repeat the process. Don't worry about getting to everyone. You can use future sessions to talk to the other group members. The important thing in this session is to make sure that whoever is telling his or her feelings is heard and that the group gives support.

Small Group No. 4: Continuing To Share Our Letters

Pick up where you left off in the previous session and continue to have the members share their letters.

If you finish, you may want to read **Romans 12:14** again, which invites us to "weep with those who weep." Invite the group to talk about how we can be of help to one another when we are hurting because of the death of someone we love.

If you have time, continue with the casket questions. Encourage your group to write more questions for the casket box. If your group is comfortable with talking about feelings, you may not have time for additional questions from the casket box. If your group is reluctant to talk about feelings, you may use the question format to deal with the issues that surround death.

Small Group No. 5: Being There for One Another

Depending on how the group sessions are going, you have several options:

1. Continue to share at a personal level and give one another support, taking as much time for each youth as needed. To give ample support may mean hearing from only one or two youth per session.
2. Use the casket box and the questions to deal with issues and questions that are important to the members of the group.
3. Move on to talking about how we can be supportive of those who feel pain and sorrow when someone they love dies.

If you chose the third option, invite the group to share how they do or do not deal with death. They may want to make a list of what helps and what doesn't help. Several of the youth may have experienced a death and may have strong reactions to how others dealt with the death or their own reaction to it. In a situation such as a death in the family, youth may be excluded or ignored. A parent or friend may get so caught up in their own grief that they become insensitive to others around them.

One possibility for this session is for each youth to write a letter to someone who has died. Another option is to write a letter that expresses what they think a deceased person would write to them if they could. A member of the group might want to hear from a deceased parent. In this case the youth would write the letter and include what they would like to hear the parent say to them.

Small Group No. 6:
Nothing Can Separate Us from the Love of God.

Invite the group members to share a time when they were really down and they felt God made a difference in their lives. You might want to begin with **Psalm 23** and invite the group to write about a time when they were "in the valley of the shadow of death" and felt God's presence.

Not everyone will have had this experience, but encourage those who have felt God's presence to tell what that was like.

Bonfire and Worship

If weather permits, spend the rest of the evening outdoors in energetic activities. Make a bonfire and cook smores (marshmallows, chocolate, and graham crackers). End with singing songs and an uplifting worship service. Use some of the Scriptures that affirm God's presence in the midst of all of life.

Free Time

Allow some time for everyone to unwind—playing informal games, talking to one another, listening to music, and talking to adults about feelings are all appropriate activities.

Field Trip to a Funeral Home

Use the time between breakfast and lunch on Sunday to take the entire group on a field trip to a funeral home. Most funeral homes will be happy to give a tour and to answer questions. Focus on the following areas that youth may be curious about:

● What does the funeral home do with the body?
● What is the role of the funeral home in a funeral?
● What function do funerals serve in our society?
● What are some funeral customs and practices?

When the tour is over, have the group go to the chapel sanctuary and do a memorial service using a funeral service that focuses on Resurrection. During the service, invite those who have lost people in the past to name the persons who have died.

Take the group out for lunch and then return to the retreat location.

Small Group No. 7: Cradle with Care

Begin by having the group discuss their thoughts and feelings about the field trip to the funeral home. Deal with any lingering questions or reactions.

Take a few minutes to process the weekend as a whole with the group. Use the following questions to guide your discussion:

- How are you feeling about the weekend right now?
- What was the most difficult thing about this retreat for you personally?
- What was the most helpful part of the weekend?
- What unresolved feelings and issues do you take with you as you leave?

Explain the "cradle with care" exercise to the group. Ask a volunteer to choose another youth who is special to him or her and to lie down face up with his or her head in that person's lap. The volunteer is to then close his or her eyes, and the rest of the group is to touch him or her on the hand, arm, or leg. The group will then go around the circle and each youth will tell how he or she feels about what the volunteer has shared during the weekend (especially noting the pain). Each youth should tell the volunteer what they hope for him or her in the future.

After the whole group has cradled the volunteer with care, the volunteer is to sit up and tell what the experience was like. Repeat the cradle activity until everyone in the group has had a chance to be the volunteer.

† Closing Worship †

Use the closing worship time for a service of thanksgiving. Focus on thanking God for the gift of life, the gift of those people who have touched our lives (living or dead), and for the love and support we experience in community.

—Walt Marcum

9

SPIRITUAL LIFE RETREAT

PURPOSE: *To help youth experience the value of quietness in their lives to balance daily activities.*

This retreat may not be for everyone in your youth fellowship. It takes some maturity to be still, to listen, and to reflect; therefore the success of the event will depend on the seriousness and the commitment of the youth.

Preparation

Make some decisions. When and where you will have the retreat? How long will it be? (If you plan to travel any distance, plan an overnight retreat.) How much will the retreat cost? Who will the adult leaders be? (Plan to have several adult leaders. If you decide to have a communion service, you will need to invite a minister.)

Decide on the activities you wish to include and delegate responsibilities for each one. Make a schedule of activities. (Feel free to change the suggested schedule.) Make a checklist of all the equipment and materials you will need.

Plan to set up a table for resources written by and for young people. Include books, magazines, and articles that contain prayers, inspirational poetry, or meditative readings. Ask your minister, education director, church librarian, or youth counselors to help find appropriate resources.

POSSIBLE SCHEDULE (1 day)

10:00 Making Notebooks
11:00 Introducing the Retreat Theme
12:00 Lunch
 1:00 Ways to Listen for Guidance
 2:00 Time Alone for Journal Writing and/or Meditation
 3:00 Party Time
 3:30 Reflective Bible Study
 4:00 Emmaus Road Guided Fantasy
 5:00 Closing Worship or Communion

Making Notebooks

The youth will need notebooks for the handouts you will give them and for journal writing, private Bible study, and other suggested activities. Ask them to use the first hour of the retreat for making notebooks. Some youth may not be sure what to expect from the retreat and may be a bit anxious. This activity may ease them into the retreat by providing a time of fellowship before the less familiar activities of meditation and reflection.

Have available materials for making notebooks: construction paper for covers, brads or yarn for fasteners, magazines or used Christmas cards for cover pictures, felt-tip markers, paper punches, rulers, scissors, glue or paste, and lined notebook paper. In addition, give the youth copies of devotional materials (prayers, inspirational poetry, short readings) to include in their notebooks. (Copies of *alive now!* might be a valuable resource.) This first hour should be a relaxed time. You may want to have tapes or records of quiet religious music playing in the background.

Introducing the Retreat Theme

Ask members of the group to sit in a semicircle facing a chalkboard or a large sheet of paper. Announce that they are going to play telephone. They are to pass a message from one person to the next, each person repeating exactly what he or she has heard. Play tapes or records of popular music at full volume. Begin the game with this message from **Isaiah 30:15**: "In quietness and in trust shall be your strength." When the message has reached the last person, turn the music off and ask the youth to report what they heard. Play the game again without music. Start a message from **Psalm 46:10**: "Be still, and know that I am God." Have youth report the message they heard. Note that they were able to hear the message more clearly without music.

Have the group discuss the following questions. List responses on a large sheet of paper

- What are some noises, pressures, or activities in our lives that drown out God's voice? (homework, school activities, jobs, pressure to make good grades and to be popular)
- What are some attitudes we hold in our society that make quiet time alone seem unacceptable? (Spending time by yourself is weird; be where the action is!)

Have everyone read **Matthew 14:22-23** and **Luke 5:15-16.** Ask:

- Why do you think Jesus prayed by himself?
- What kinds of pressures do you think Jesus had to deal with in his life?
- How active a person do you think he was?

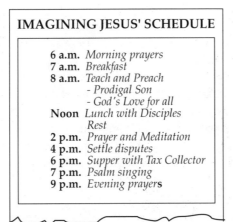

IMAGINING JESUS' SCHEDULE

6 a.m.	*Morning prayers*
7 a.m.	*Breakfast*
8 a.m.	*Teach and Preach*
	- Prodigal Son
	- God's Love for all
Noon	*Lunch with Disciples*
	Rest
2 p.m.	*Prayer and Meditation*
4 p.m.	*Settle disputes*
6 p.m.	*Supper with Tax Collector*
7 p.m.	*Psalm singing*
9 p.m.	*Evening prayers*

Ask the group to develop a daily schedule that they think Jesus might have followed. Suggest that the schedule include times for getting up, going to bed, working, eating, relaxing, teaching, and so on. Write the schedule on a large sheet of paper.

When the group has finished this activity, invite the youth to write in their notebooks their own daily schedules. The schedules should include as much quiet time as the youth feel is necessary and possible for them.

Ways to Listen for Guidance

Print the following items on separate sheets of paper and post them in various places around the room. Each item is numbered (from 2-7) and includes a Bible reference and a question.

2. **James 1:5-8** What kind of prayer would you say?
3. **Proverbs 20:5** What do you think your friend is thinking or feeling?
4. **Colossians 3:12-14** What does this passage say to you about your situation?
5. **Luke 6:27-28** What does this passage say about your situation?
6. **Matthew 5:23-24** How might you make peace with your friend?
7. Look over what you have written. Be alone for a while and ask for God's guidance. Sit in silence until a course of action becomes clear to you. Write it down.

Make copies of the following situation and give each person a copy.

You have a good friend whom you have known for a long time. You are in the same grade at the same school. You go to the same church and are active in the youth group. You are always together. Then your friend suddenly starts going to another church that is very different from yours. He or she insists that your church is wrong and wants you to go to his or her church. You visit but don't feel it's the church for you. You tell your friend how you feel. Your friend will no longer do things with you. You are troubled by this and need some guidance about what to do.

Ask the youth to number from 1 to 7 in their notebooks leaving several lines of space between the numbers. Ask them to read the situation silently and to write by number 1 their answer to the question, What would you do in this situation? The youth should write the first answer that comes to mind.

Then tell the youth that there are Bible references placed around the room. They are to read the Bible verses and write in their notebooks, next to the corresponding number, their answers to the questions. They can start with any of the references except number 7, which they must do last. Ask them to do this whole activity in silence.

When all the youth have finished, call the group together and ask: "How many of you wrote a different answer for number 7 than for number 1?" Have the youth discuss what they would do in the situation described and decide, as a group, on the best course of action. Then ask: "What have you learned from this activity? What are some ways to find guidance for problems?" List answers so that youth can copy them into their notebooks.

Party Time

If you have an overnight retreat, a party will balance an afternoon of study and reflection. Include both active, noisy games and quiet games. Plan "Party Time" so that the last activities will help youth to settle down and to be ready for the "Emmaus Walk Guided Fantasy." You may want to sing a quiet song or two after the last game to create a mood for the fantasy experience.

Reflective Bible Study

Give a copy of the following material to each person. Divide the youth into small groups of no more than eight people. "Reflective Bible Study" should be done alone. When all the members of a small group are finished, they may want to talk about their answers.

Reflective Bible Study

Read silently **Mark 4:35-41**. As you read, try to imagine that you are with Jesus and his disciples.

- What do you see?
- What do you hear?
- What do you feel with your fingers or on your skin?
- What are the emotions you feel?

When everyone in the group has finished this section, you may talk about your answers.
   Relate the biblical experience to your own life. Write down brief answers to the following questions:

1. When has an experience in your life suddenly changed from calm to storm?
2. When in your life have you said to God, "Don't you care about what's happening to me?"
3. When in your life have you been calm within yourself in the midst of a stormy situation? How did this happen?
4. What lines in this passage relate to your present experience?

Emmaus Road Guided Fantasy

Read the following directions to the youth. Give them plenty of time to do each activity before you read the next one. Do not rush this activity.

1. Find a comfortable place to sit or lie down apart from other persons.
2. Close your eyes and relax.
3. Breathe slowly and concentrate on your breathing.
4. Imagine. You and a close friend are going for a walk together. Choose your friend. Choose a place to walk.
5. Tell your friend about a concern you have. Take your time.

6. Now you are suddenly joined by a wise person who asks what you have been talking about. Imagine what the wise person looks like.

7. Tell the wise person about your conversation.

8. Listen to what he or she says to you.

9. You have now reached your house. Invite the wise person in to join you and your friend for refreshments.

10. As you sit down, ask the wise person to offer a blessing.

11. When you open your eyes after the blessing, the wise person has disappeared but on the table is a gift. What is it?

12. When you are ready, open your eyes.

13. Write about your experiences in your notebooks.

Journal Writing

Give each person a copy of the following material.

Journal Writing

A journal is a personal, written reflection. What you write is between you and God, and you will not be asked to read it or tell about it. You are therefore free to write whatever you wish—your thoughts, your feelings, your personal insights. You don't need to worry about grammar, spelling, or sentence structure. Here are some ways to get started.

1. *Reflect on the past day or week.* Write down the big things that happened to you. Which ones do you feel good about? Why? Which ones do you wish had been different? What could you have done to make them different? What have you learned from the day's or the week's experiences? Write down your answers and reflect on them. Ask God to help you act on what you have learned.

2. *Write down how you are feeling right now (happy, lonely, peaceful, angry,and so forth).* What has happened to make you feel this way? Who are the people and what are the experiences that have triggered these feelings?What is within you that causes you to respond in this way? Write down your answers and reflect on them. Ask God to help you be in charge of your emotions and use them creatively.

3. *Read slowly and reflectively a Scripture passage, a prayer, the words of a hymn, or a short devotional.* Before you read, take a moment to be quiet and to ask God's help in understanding what you read and in applying it to your life. After you read, ask yourself: In what ways does this reading relate to my experience or my character? Write down your thoughts. Reflect on what you have written. Ask God to help you respond to any insights that may require you to act or to change.

Finding Help in the Bible

Give a copy of the following to each person. This material is to be used for private Bible study.

Finding Help in the Bible

Read:
    Matthew 6:25-34 when you are worried;
    Mark 10:35-45 when you want to be important;
    I John 1:8-11 when things go wrong and you are tempted to blame other people;
    Psalm 23 when you are lonely or afraid;
    Romans 8:31-39 when someone you love dies;
    I Peter 3:13-17 when it is hard to do what you feel is right;
    Romans 12:14-18 when you have trouble getting along with people
    Philippians 3:12-16 when you are too discouraged to try again;
    Hebrews 12:5-11 when you feel your parents are unfair;
    I Corinthians 13:1-7 when you have a fight or disagreement with someone you care about.

How to Meditate

Give a copy of the following material to each person.

How to Meditate

Meditation is one of the most difficult forms of prayer. It involves being silent, ridding the mind of all distractions, and focusing on God alone. When a person meditates, he or she does not ask anything of God except to be in God's presence. Following are some suggestions to help you meditate.

1. Find a place where you can be alone.
2. Sit in a comfortable position, but not so comfortable that you go to sleep. You need to stay alert.
3. Close your eyes and relax. Start with the top of your head and relax each part of your body, imagining that the tension is draining out through the bottom of your feet.
4. Breathe in and out very slowly. As you do so, repeat a mantra, concentrating on the word or words as you breathe in and out. A mantra is a word or phrase that helps you keep your mind focused on God: God, Lord Jesus, peace, love, God is love, be still, be still and know. Choose whatever word or phrase is most meaningful to you. You may want to say the mantra aloud at first and gradually soften your voice until you are repeating it to yourself.
5. Another way of focusing is to imagine something like a candle, a flower, or your image of Jesus.
6. When your mind starts to wander, focus your attention on the word or phrase or image you have chosen.
7. Listen to what God is saying to you in the silence. What God says may come to you as a thought, a phrase, or an image.
8. When you have finished your meditation, write in your notebook what you experienced and reflect on it.

✝   Closing Worship   ✝

The following worship resources can be used to create a worship service for a retreat.

Hymns:
Breathe on Me, Breath of God
Kum Ba Yah
Lord, I Want to be a Christian,
Seek Ye First the Kingdom of God
Spirit of God, Descend on My Heart
Spirit of the Living God

Scripture:
Psalms 139:1-12, 23, 24 (presence of God everywhere)
Matthew 6:31-33 (seek first the kingdom of God)
Matthew 13:31-33, 44-46 (parables of the kingdom of God)
Luke 11:9-10 (ask, seek, knock)
17:20-21 (kingdom of God is among us)

—Georgianna Summers

10

HOW CAN I BE FRIENDS WITH SOMEONE WHO IS LOCKED UP?

PURPOSE: *To help youth learn how to relate to their peers who are involved in institutional care (jails, juvenile detention centers, drug rehabilitation centers, and counseling facilities).*

Youth need to face the reality of institutional intervention into the lives of their friends and peers. This intervention may take a variety of shapes and may be short-term or long-term. It may be on a voluntary or an involuntary basis. It may involve twenty-four hour supervision, night lockup only, or daytime outpatient care. Before their eighteenth birthday, many youth will have a friend or peer in some kind of institutional care. Youth will be aware that the peer experiencing institutional intervention is someone in deep need. The youth may want to help, but they may not know what help is appropriate. Knowing someone in institutional care may cause the youth to feel fearful for the possibility of their own institutionalization. They need to understand institutionalization, to know how to listen to an institutionalized peer in a non-judgmental, supportive way, and to be able to approach the whole situation without an attitude of fear. Long before the event takes place, those who will lead this event need to set aside a time to discuss thoroughly their own feelings about these and other related issues.

This event offers a number of different ways to sample the experience of being institutionalized. The event includes field experiences in which youth will actually travel to institutions to meet staff and residents. The event also includes an overnight lock-in, in where the expressing of ideas and feelings will be encouraged. The retreat offers a brief, mild, lockup simulation and offers the opportunity to reflect on the experience of being locked up. You will have an opportunity for question and answer sessions with persons directly involved in institutional care. Roleplaying has been designed to help youth relate to peers undergoing institutional care.

Preparation

Have one adult supervisor or counselor for every four to five youth. Adults need to make a commitment to a twenty-four hour, overnight period of time. Each adult should be a licensed driver and should have a vehicle available for the event.

Due to the nature of the event, inform parents about the purpose of the event and the activities you will be leading, including the fact that visits to institutions will be involved. A concise, printed, parent or guardian permission slip should be distributed directly to the parent(s) or guardian(s) several weeks before the event. Before the event, the signed permission slip must be in the hands of the youth leaders.

Secure adequate space for an overnight stay. Space in the church building would be a good choice. Schedule the use of the church early to avoid conflict with other congregational activities. Make arrangements for supper and breakfast at the church. You might ask parents to be responsible for planning and preparing the meals. Resist the temptation to go out to a fast-food place for meals. Leaving the building for meals will interfere with the flow and with the mood of the event.

At least one month prior to the event, determine what kind of institutional intervention is most prevalent in your community. To find this information, ask school counselors, city or county juvenile officers, city or county law enforcement officials, juvenile detention center officials, officials in detoxification centers, and so on. These persons can tell you where the youth of the area are generally sent for both voluntary and involuntary care. Involuntary care means that the youth is placed in the facility by court mandate or other legal procedures, with or without willingness to go. Find facilities to which peers of the youth are most often sent. Arrange a time to visit both a voluntary and an involuntary facility. The officials of the facility will usually be co-operative in scheduling visits and in helping your group understand the purpose of their institution. Be sure the officials understand that you are interested in knowing how youth can minister to other youth who are institutionalized. If possible, invite a staff person and a resident from each type of facility in your area to meet with the group on the second day of the event. What is expected of these four people, as outlined in the next session, should be thoroughly explained.

Have one adult leader present for the entire event. This leader might be your pastor or a qualified, professional counselor, with skills in listening to youth and in helping them deal with their fears. Youth will likely experience fear and anxiety as they deal with this unsettling area of life, and it is essential to have someone on hand to help them deal with their fears. The pastor or counselor should be ready to offer formal and informal support, both in group and in individual situations.

POSSIBLE SCHEDULE (2 days)

SATURDAY

    12:00 Gathering
    12:45 Introduce purpose of retreat
     1:00 Opening worship
     1:15 Visit institutions
     5:30 Supper
     7:00 Recreation
     8:00 Simulation lock-up
    10:30 Evening devotions

SUNDAY

     7:00 Morning devotions
     7:30 Breakfast
     8:30 Youth share stories
    10:00 Listening skills
    11:15 Closing worship

DAY 1

Gather at the church at noon. Ahead of time, ask everyone involved to eat lunch before they arrive. Begin the day with a time of worship. The focus of the worship should be on the legitimate concerns and anxieties all persons have about the event. Claiming the presence and power of the Holy Spirit to help us know what to say, how to act, and how to deal with fears should be included in the worship. (**Matthew 10:17-22** is one text that promises the power of the Spirit for tough times.) Also, include some words of hope and expectation about the event.

Lead the youth group in reading **Matthew 25:36.** Then, ask a youth to read **Matthew 25:31-46.** Ask the group:

● Have you ever known anyone who was in prison or in another institution?
● How did you feel about that person?
● How was that person treated by the community?
● How did you treat that person?

Say: "It's easy to be embarrassed, to not know what to do or to say or how to deal with a person who is or has been in an institution. Our immediate reaction is to pretend nothing happened, or to pretend the person doesn't exist." Ask: "Is that what Jesus meant when he talked about visiting those in prison? How do we treat someone as if he or she were Jesus? If we knew Jesus was in prison, what would we do?"

Tell the group about what they will see and experience at the institutions. Answer any questions you can, and deal with concerns that are raised. Probably, most concerns will be about how persons should act. If you do not have a good feel for how to answer that question, tell youth that you will raise that question with the personnel at the institution before the visit begins. Travel in groups of four or five, with adults driving each vehicle, to each of the institutions you have arranged to visit. At each institution, put yourselves in the hands of the personnel who will be leading you. They will be happy to deal with any questions or concerns your group may have. The chief responsibility and concern of the institution personnel is for the persons with whom they work in the facility, so they will also be concerned about how your group acts while visiting.

Following the visit, return to the church or wherever you are spending the night. Discuss with the group what they saw and heard. The pastor, counselor, or other helping professional who has been secured for the event, should lead the discussion. This leader should help group members talk openly about the parts of the visits and the elements of institutionalization that frightened them or that made them feel anxious. Youth should be encouraged by the counselor to talk with him or her privately about their fears if they feel the need to do so. Fears and anxieties may be a dominant part of the discussion, but some positive feelings will also be present. Close the discussion with prayer for the group and for their feelings, for the persons who are institutionalized, and for the persons who work in the institutions.

Following the discussion, break for supper and some free time, followed by organized recreation. Times of strong feelings should be followed by active games to help release tension.

After supper and recreation, ask for youth volunteers to participate in a lockup. Set aside two hours for youth volunteers to be locked up in isolation. This represents a brief simulation of the isolation persons can feel in an institution. Rooms for the lockup should be small. To make the simulation more authentic, remove all the familiar furniture, pictures, and so forth from the room. If there is a problem with removing furniture or pictures from the room, then remove any books or other means of passing the time. Lock the doors to the room if possible. If the rooms do not have locks, close the doors and post a guard or guards in the hallway.

This activity is voluntary. You need to know in advance how many rooms to prepare, so ask group members to sign up for the lockup activity when they register for the event. Allow anyone to change his or her mind about participating in this event. For those who do not want to participate in this event, provide an option. Perhaps a film dealing with some type of youth institutionalization could be shown. Be sure you have previewed the movie and that it is suitable for your group.

After the lockup, bring the whole group together. Encourage group members who endured the lockup to talk about how they felt being confined in one place and being denied access to their regular group. Group members who watched the film could share their feelings about observing persons who are institutionalized.

Close the evening with a devotional time. You may want to use **Acts 12:1-5** as part of the devotional. Since the evening has been so intense, be flexible about bed times. Give the youth an opportunity to unwind and blow off steam, but do insist on a certain amount of rest in preparation for the next day.

DAY 2

Begin the second day with breakfast and a devotional time.

Following the morning devotion, ask to hear from youth who are or have been involved in voluntary and involuntary institutional care. Allow the youth to tell their stories and to make any remarks they wish to make. When the youth have finished their stories, the other youth may ask questions.

The group will then hear from an institution official or a panel of officials. The focus should be on the listening skills necessary when visiting or communicating with a peer who is institutionalized. Have a roleplay concerning visits to a person who is institutionalized. Ask a youth volunteer to be a visitor to someone who is locked-up, while an institutional official plays the role of someone who is institutionalized. Allow the official to set the stage. Following the roleplay, discuss what has occurred, then evaluate what can be learned about listening skills. After the roleplay, the youth and the leaders will divide into pairs, alternately roleplaying a visitor and an institutionalized person.

† Closing Worship †

Close the event by rereading **Matthew 25:36.** Ask the group members to think of and to write down a specific way they will deal with an institutionalized person with the assumption that they are dealing directly with Jesus. These commitments might take the form of:

● visiting the institutionalized person
● visiting the parents of the institutionalized person
● writing letters
● sending care packages
● saying prayers

Invite youth to tell their commitments to the group. Give personal affirmation to each youth and offer a closing prayer asking God's blessing on the commitments. Thank the guests, and clean the facility prior to dismissal.

—Geoff Posegate

11

AM I IN THE CLUTCHES OF AN ISM?

PURPOSE: *To help youth identify and clarify their own attitudes toward racism, sexism, ageism, handicappism, and cliqueism and to move toward being more aware and sensitive to those around them.*

Plan for a twenty-four-hour, overnight retreat in your local church or in a camp or retreat center. The retreat event will provide an opportunity for youth to focus on some of their own feelings and behaviors toward others. It will also provide a setting to explore these thoughts and behaviors in relation to the biblical Golden Rule (**Luke 6:31**).

Preparation

Several weeks before the event, form small groups of both adults and youth to plan and carry out the retreat. If your group is small, ask everyone to sign up for more than one committee. Schedule definite times for the committees to meet. Appoint one youth and one adult to be co-directors of the retreat and to coordinate the work of all the committees.

Find and reserve the place for the retreat. Determine the cost of the retreat per person, make registration and permission forms, and set a deadline for registration. Make house rules for the retreat, arrive early at the site to help others settle in, and be in charge of a clean-up schedule which involves everyone's participation at some time during the twenty-four hours. Provide a folder for each person containing a retreat schedule and a place to keep other handouts from the retreat.

Invite persons who have personal experiences with racism, sexism, ageism, handicappism, and cliqueism to speak at the first evening gathering. Prepare a list of questions or topics that youth would like the speakers to discuss. Explain the format and time limit to the guest speakers.

Do to others as you would have them do to you.
—Luke 6:31

POSSIBLE SCHEDULE (2 days)

FRIDAY EVENING
- 5:00 Settling in
- 5:30 Welcome and introductions
  - Opening ice breaker game
  - Theme of the retreat
  - Evening devotions
- 6:00 Dinner
  - Group singing
  - Clean up and free time
- 7:00 What is an *ism*?
  - Guest speakers
  - Group discussion
- 8:00 Social hour and refreshments
- 9:00 Movie
- 11:00 Lights out

SATURDAY
- 7:00 Wake up
- 7:30 Breakfast
- 8:00 Clean up
- 8:30 Morning devotions
- 9:00 Group singing
  - Movie review and discussion
  - Recap definition of *ism*
- 9:30 Small group discussion and Bible study
- 10:30 Group reports
- 11:00 Rally sign making
- 12:00 Lunch and free time
- 1:00 Awareness raising activities
- 3:00 Tying it together
  - Group singing
  - Closing worship
- 5:00 On the way home

Recreation and Group Singing

Lead the opening ice breaker game and provide music and/or games for the social hour during the first evening. Be responsible for having sports equipment and indoor game equipment available for the free time scheduled. Find a song leader to lead group singing or rotate the responsibility among the committee members. Provide song books or song sheets and choose fun songs for the event.

For the opening ice breaker game, have available enough paper and pencils for each youth. Provide a large sheet of paper and markers for group activity. Ask the youth to get into pairs, and have each youth in the pair tell the other youth a word he or she knows that ends in the suffix *ism*. (If players do not know one another, have them introduce themselves each time they form a pair or group.) Each youth may write only the word given by the other person. Tell the pairs to separate and to find two other people. Each youth must think of another *ism* word and give it to the other two youth to write. Each youth is to write two new words. Tell the pairs to separate and ask each youth to find three other youth to get two new *ism* words from. The pairs may continue to separate as long as each youth finds two new *ism* words each time, or until there are no longer any other youth to form a group. When a pair can no longer come up with new words, they must sit down and wait for the other pairs to finish. When all the pairs are finished, pass out the markers and ask each youth to write one *ism* word on the large piece of paper such as:

baptism communism ageism heroism sexism materialism racism

Retreat Theme

Say to the group: Our society is full of *isms*. Some carry positive feelings and others carry negative feelings. However, when those *isms* in our society carry only negative feelings and lots of people respond negatively, then our society can be said to be suffering from a social illness. Our society is in the clutch of an *ism*.

Most of the time we don't think about discrimination. We may know that it exists, we may see it now and then, but we don't often think very long about it, or *do* anything about it. When we do see some sort of discrimination, we often don't know how to respond. We know that racism is against the teachings of Jesus. We know that we need to treat our elderly with respect and dignity. We know that we need to work at eliminating sex stereotypes in many areas of our life. We know that we need to accept all people with handicapping conditions as full members in our society. Between knowing and doing, however, we may fall into a great gray area called an *ism*.

Racism, sexism, ageism, and handicappism are the major *isms* to be discussed during the retreat. Cliqueism has been coined as an *ism* word and has been included here because it, more than any other *ism*, pervades the youth experience. *Cliqueism*, at some time or other, affects everyone. By looking at *isms* during our retreat, we can become more aware of our own feelings and should be able to make a commitment to more peaceful relations wherever we may be.

Movie

Choose a movie that is appropriate to the theme and that will stimulate discussion on one of the isms being discussed at the retreat. Preview the movie and formulate a movie review sheet for each person to fill out for group discussion the following morning. Provide the necessary equipment to show the movie. Show the movie on the first evening, and lead a group discussion about the movie. Possible movies might include the following:

Age: *On Golden Pond* or *Sunshine Boys*
Race: *To Kill a Mockingbird, Guess Who's Coming to Dinner?*
Cliques: *Can't Buy Me Love*
Sexism: *Just One of the Guys*
Handicappism: *Butterflies Are Free*

Use the following discussion questions:

- What year was this movie made?
- What issues about *isms* did it raise?
- How did the movie deal with the *ism*?
- If a movie were made today about this topic, would it reflect any progress toward social awareness in the last twenty years? ten years? five years?

Awareness Activities

Plan at least one awareness raising activity for each of the five *isms* and provide a rotating schedule so that all the participants have a chance to experience each activity during the two-hour session on the second afternoon. Gather the necessary materials, lead the activities, or find qualified adults to lead the activities. The group may want to design their own activities or use the suggestions that follow.

Racism

Set a simple restaurant scene with two tables and chairs. As people come to the restaurant and wait to be seated, discriminate on color issues. For example, when the first group comes, seat only those who have blue eyes and make the others wait; or seat only those who have white tennis shoes on and make the others wait; or seat only those with black hair and make the others wait. Change the discrimination factor for each group. Have someone play the role of the manager. This person will have to explain the restaurant's policy each time someone questions why they are not being seated. Spend time talking about how the participants felt during this exercise. Invite the students to share other personal observations of racism.

Sexism

Set up an office for interviewing job applicants. Provide a list of job openings and application forms. Have each person fill out an application form and present it to an interviewer. Have the interviewer go over the person's application and then no matter what the job is or what the person's qualifications are, the interviewer must turn down the applicant because he or she is the wrong sex for the job. Talk about whether this ever happens today. Discuss other areas where sexism is noticed.

Ageism

Invite someone who knows how to do theater make-up to make-up persons as if they were older than they are. If a professional is not available, provide theater make-up and let each person experiment with a partner. Provide clean-up materials. Discuss: Do you ever think about what it will be like to grow old? Do you approve or disapprove of the way our society cares for its elderly population?

Handicappism

Borrow or rent two wheelchairs. Give each person an opportunity to try an activity such as dancing, playing ball, gaining entrance into the building or restroom, or racing through an obstacle course. While two people are using the wheelchairs, provide other activities that a person who is blind, deaf, or who has some other handicapping condition might experience.

Cliqueism

Play the game "wanna be" to elicit those feelings associated with being on the *in* or *out* with a popular clique. Have everyone sit in a circle. Ask for three or four volunteers who want to be in the clique to leave the room. Have the remaining youth decide what kind of clique they are by choosing an animal to express their identity. For example, is the group angry like a dog; arrogant like a cat; slippery like a fish; and so on.

Invite the volunteers back into the room. Have the volunteers, one by one, ask the group a question about the clique's identity. Every youth in the clique takes turns answering the questions with either yes or no. While the verbal answer must either be yes or no, the youth answering may use body language or a tone of voice that would give clues. The questioning continues until one of the wanna be's successfully guesses the group's identity. Play continues as time allows with different people who wanna be leaving the room each time. Spend time discussing the cliques that are in the students' schools or churches. Discuss this statement: Cliques serve a good social purpose.

Bible Study

Prepare a study sheet for each participant. Divide the group into five small groups with each group discussing one of the five *isms* (racism, sexism, ageism, handicappism, cliqueism). The study sheet might include the following, with spaces between for students to write their own thoughts:
1. Read the Golden Rule as it is found in **Luke 6:31**. Write it down.
2. List five things you know about this group's *ism*.
3. List the positive ways our society has dealt with this *ism*.
4. List ways that our society could better deal with this *ism*.
5. If Jesus were attending your group study and he told you the Golden Rule, what do you think he would mean for you to do in detail when you meet a person who appears to be different from you?
6. Have you ever used the Golden Rule as a guide for your behavior? If so, when? Was this a good rule to follow in your situation?
7. Do you think the Golden Rule could be helpful, should be helpful, can be helpful, or cannot be helpful toward more peaceful relations among people in school, in churches, in communities, and in nations of the world?

Rally Signs

The rally signs may be used during the closing worship and then taken home. You will need the following materials for the rally signs:

- posterboard or cardboard boxes which can be cut up into rally signs about 1½ by 2 feet
- scrap lumber for handles
- felt-tip markers or poster paints
- large staplers

Ask each youth to make their own rally sign on the theme of the retreat. Encourage them to include the Golden Rule in their own words and to show, with pictures or words, what that means to them in relation to one or all of the *isms* discussed during the retreat. Direct the youth to include a statement or picture which would affirm their new awareness or to include an affirmation showing how their behavior to others might be different.

Worship

The evening devotions before dinner should be very short. Plan a few words and a prayer to focus on the retreat's purpose of becoming more aware and sensitive to those around us who appear to be different. For the morning devotions, prepare or ask an adult to prepare a mini-talk or to tell a story relating to the retreat theme. Include some thoughts about how our awareness concerning others who are different from us is reflected in how we act toward them (from ignoring them to teasing them and all the behaviors in between). For the closing worship, see the following section, or plan your own closing worship to include tying together all the pieces of the retreat, affirming a new awareness toward others, and celebrating the retreat event.

✝   Closing Worship   ✝

Before the retreat, gather enough old bricks so that there will be one for each participant. If bricks are unavailable, use any type of material that can be used to build a wall such as shoe boxes or scrap lumber. Using felt-tip markers, write on each brick an *ism* word or a negative feeling that *isms* create. Before the worship service, build a wall with the bricks in the worship area where everyone can gather around. Invite everyone to bring their rally sign to the closing worship. Provide a liturgy for each person. Ask one youth and one adult to prepare mini-sermons to bring all the thoughts of the retreat together.

LEADER: As we gather around the brick wall we are more aware than ever of the barriers that *isms* create between people. We are more aware than ever that it is up to each of us to break down the wall of misinformation and the wall of apathy and fear which helps this wall stand.

RESPONSE: We will take our new awareness with us as we go today and commit ourselves to breaking down the wall of *isms* in our society. (Each participant should take one brick away from the wall.)

LEADER: Becoming aware of our feelings and the feelings of others around us will help break down the wall of *isms*. We will stop and consider our thoughts and behaviors in light of the Golden Rule whenever we are with others who appear to be different from ourselves.

RESPONSE: We will plant our new awareness in the place where the old brick wall stood. We will think about the Golden Rule as a guide for our thoughts and behavior towards others who appear to be different from us. (Each participant should take their rally sign and lay it in the place where the brick wall stood. If this is outside, have them plant their sign in the ground.)

LEADER: We celebrate our time together to learn, to share our feelings, to grow in our awareness, to have fun, and to worship together. We leave today asking God's guidance.

RESPONSE: We celebrate our time together and take our new awareness to our homes, to our schools, and to the streets of our communities. We commit ourselves to more peaceful relations among all people everywhere.

CLOSING HYMN AND BENEDICTION

—Elizabeth Brower

12

RELATING TO PERSONS WITH A HANDICAPPING CONDITION

PURPOSE: *To help youth understand what it means to have handicapping conditions and discover ways of being open to persons with handicapping conditions.*

Though "Relating to Persons with Handicapping Conditions" can be used alone, it is best used as preparation for ministry with persons who have handicapping conditions. Encourage the group to think about the event as a step toward ministry with and to persons with handicapping conditions.

Preparation

Begin to prepare for the event several weeks ahead of time. Read through the program. As you read the program, make a list of all the materials you will need and be sure they are available. If members of the youth group have handicapping conditions, talk with them before the event to find out if they plan to attend. Be open to their feelings about the event and about the activities you've planned. Try to involve them in preparing for the event. Ask if they have ideas for other activities that would help the group better understand what it means to deal with handicapping conditions. They may want to prepare a presentation about the difficulties they face, their feelings about having handicapping conditions, the way they want to be treated by others in the group, and so forth.

The event includes having two guest speakers. One of the speakers should be a person with handicapping conditions, the other a counselor, social worker, or interpreter who works with persons with handicapping conditions. Invite the speakers at least two weeks before the event; tell them what you want them to talk about and how long they will have for their presentations. In addition, invite your pastor to attend the event and to prepare a service of liberation and healing.

POSSIBLE SCHEDULE (2 days)

FRIDAY EVENING
- 7:00 Arrival
- 7:20 Welcome and introduction
- 7:30 Forced Choice Exercise
- 8:15 Small Group Discussion
- 9:00 Ice Cream Sundaes
- 10:00 Worship
- 10:30 Free Time
- 11:00 Lights Out

SATURDAY
- 8:00 Communication Check-in; Simulated Handicapping Conditions
- 9:00 Breakfast
- 10:00 Bible Study
- 10:45 Compare Bible Studies
- 11:45 Making Lunch
- 12:30 Lunch
- 1:15 Cleanup
- 1:45 Guest Speaker: A Personal Witness
- 3:00 Recreation
- 4:00 Making Dinner
- 4:45 Dinner
- 5:30 Cleanup
- 6:15 Worship
- 7:00 Small Groups
- 7:45 Guest Speaker
- 8:45 Group Time
- 9:30 Closing Prayer Circle
- 10:00 Pack Up and Return Home

Forced Choice Exercise

This activity is an introduction to the theme of the event. It is a forced choice exercise in which participants will be asked to reflect on how much value they place on their physical and mental capabilities. Explain to the youth that you will ask several questions and that you will instruct them to go to one part of the room or another depending on their response to each question. After the youth respond to each question, ask them to explain their responses. If members of the group have handicapping conditions, be especially sensitive to their feelings. Read the following:

1. *Which of your senses do you value the most:* sight, hearing, or touch? Go to the right side of the room if you think sight is the most valuable, the left side of the room if you most value your hearing, and the middle of the room if you choose touch.
2. *Which do you value the most:* your intellectual capacities, your physical capabilities, or your emotions? If you most value your intellect, go to the right side of the room; if your physical capabilities, go to the left side of the room; if your emotions, go to the middle of the room.
3. *Which of your senses would you prefer to lose:* sight, hearing, or touch? If you would prefer to lose your sight, go to the right side of the room, if your hearing, go to the left side of the room, if your touch, go to the middle of the room.
4. *Which of the following losses would be the most difficult to accept:* speech because of a stroke, physical capabilities because of a heart condition, or mental abilities because of Alzheimer's disease? If you think losing your speech would be the most difficult, go to the right side of the room; if losing your physical capabilities would be the most difficult, go to the left side of the room; if losing your mental abilities would be the most difficult, go to the middle of the room.

5. *Which would be the least difficult for you:* paralysis of your hands, your legs, or your face and tongue? Go to the right side of the room if losing the ability to move your hands would be the least difficult, to the left side of the room if losing the ability to move your legs would be the least difficult, to the middle of the room if losing the ability to move your face and tongue would be the least difficult.

Small Groups: Discuss the Exercise

Have the youth divide into small groups. They will work in the same small groups later in the event. Invite the groups to talk about the forced choice exercise. Ask: Which of your capabilities are most important to you? Why? In what ways do you take your capabilities for granted?

Make Your Own Ice Cream Sundaes

Have available all the ingredients for making sundaes: ice cream, toppings, nuts, whipped cream, bowls, spoons, napkins. Encourage the youth to make their own sundaes.

Worship

Invite the youth to participate in a service of worship. Use a service you or the youth create. You may want to use the following order:

Hymns
Scripture Readings: **Psalm 22:22-32** or **1 John 4:7-12**
Prayer of Thanksgiving
Message: The Blessings of Good Health and Well-Being
Prayers for Persons Who Are Ill or Who Suffer
Hymn: "Take My Life, and Let It Be" or "We Are a Rainbow"

Simulated Handicapping Conditions

Before the simulation game, establish rules for communication. For the rest of the day, some members of the group will be unable to hear, see, or speak. Ask the group to make decisions about how they will communicate with one another so that everyone will be included. List rules of communication on a chalkboard or a large sheet of paper. One or two adult leaders should monitor conversations for the rest of the day.

Assign each person a handicapping condition. Instruct the youth to simulate blindness with gauze eye patches and a blindfold and deafness with small sponge ear plugs. They can use strips of cloth to immobilize their arms, crutches and wheelchairs to simulate paralysis, large ace bandages to immobilize their fingers and hands. Think of ways to simulate other handicapping conditions. If a member of the group has a handicapping condition, use care assigning him or her another one.

Explain to the group that they will have to deal with their simulated handicaps for the rest of the day and that they should take them seriously. Some teens will get silly with this activity, especially at first. Others will want to take a break from their handicapping condition. Repeat the purpose of the activity and encourage the youth to remember those who cannot ''take a break'' from their conditions.

Safety is also an important factor. Ask the youth to be aware of potential hazards, but do not remove them. Persons with crutches have to contend with steps, and sharp corners do not disappear in the homes of persons who are blind. Encourage the group to be aware of potential hazards; ask them to be ready to help if they are asked or if they see another person in danger. Having to ask for help or having to wait for help is part of learning about and becoming more sensitive to persons with handicapping conditions.

Give the youth time to become adjusted to their assigned handicapping conditions.

Bible Study

The Scripture should be presented and discussed in several different ways so that it is available to persons with simulated handicaps. One of the youth might pantomime the Scripture as another reads it. Or they may want to write the Scripture on a chalkboard or a large sheet of paper to make it accessible to people who are deaf.

Unfortunately, Scripture is sometimes misused in ways that are insensitive or oppressive. Try to avoid religious extremes. Some people say that if a person with a handicapping condition just prays hard enough, he or she will be miraculously cured. Others say that God must have wanted people to have handicapping conditions. Many people came to Jesus with questions and beliefs that linked illness with sin and implied that if a person were sinful, he or she would be sick and if a person were sick, he or she must have been sinful.

Have available enough Bibles for everyone and Bible commentaries on Mark and 2 Corinthians.

Have the youth divide into small groups to read **Mark 5:25-34, Mark 7:31-37,** or **2 Corinthians 12:1-10** and to discuss the following questions:

- What was Jesus' response to the person with a handicapping condition?
- How did the person approach Jesus Christ?
- Did a healing take place? If so, how? If not, why?
- What is the importance of touch in the healing process?
- Was the person healed in public or private? Why?
- What does the story say to us about our ministry to others?

Remind the youth to be aware of persons in their small groups who are unable to speak, see, or hear. Write the questions on a chalkboard or large sheet of paper and post them where everyone can see them.

Compare Bible Studies

Bring the groups together to compare the three Bible passages. Ask each group to report on their discussion in ways that all of the youth can understand. Remind them of their communication rules.

Making Lunch and Dinner

Making lunch and dinner are fairly simple tasks that may be difficult for persons with handicapping conditions. The youth will experience some of the difficulties of having handicaps and some of the necessary adjustments individuals with handicapping conditions must make in order to cope with everyday tasks. Require the youth to do as much as they can for themselves and to cooperate with one another in preparing meals and cleaning up afterward.

Guest Speaker: A Personal Witness

Invite a person with handicapping conditions to speak to the group. Someone in your church may be willing to come. Or contact community self-help groups, associations for persons with specific handicapping conditions (associations for the blind, the deaf, and so forth), Veterans Administration hospitals, or veterans associations and request the names of individuals who might be willing to speak with your group.

Ask the speaker to tell about his or her feelings about having handicapping conditions, about the challenges of daily living, and about how other people relate to him or her. The guest speaker may choose to talk about support he or she has received from other people or groups. Be sure to tell your guest how much time he or she will have for his or her presentation and for questions and answers afterward.

Recreation

Remind the youth that the purpose of the event is to help them become more sensitive to persons with handicapping conditions by understanding some of the difficulties they face. Organize relay races, hide and seek, or volleyball. Teens will keep their handicapping conditions during recreation.

Worship: Liberation and Healing Service

At least a month before this event, ask your youth minister or pastor to prepare a service of liberation and healing. Give him or her a copy of "Relating to Persons with Handicapping Conditions" and explain the purpose of the event and the worship service. Practically, the service of liberation and healing will be a time when the youth give up their simulated handicaps. However, the emphasis of the service should not be on miraculous healing; persons with real handicaps do not always have the option of being healed. Rather, the worship service should be a celebration of the group's new spirit and their new attitudes toward persons with handicapping conditions.

Small Groups: Unpacking Your Feelings

Have the youth divide into the same small groups to talk about their experience of having simulated handicaps. Ask: How did you feel about having a handicapping condition? How did you feel about having to ask for help? In what ways did other people treat you differently because of your condition? In what ways did you change in order to adjust to having a handicapping condition? Before this event, what were your attitudes or beliefs about persons with handicapping conditions? How were your attitudes changed? What have you learned?

Guest Speaker: Workers with Persons Who Have Handicapping Conditions

Invite someone who works with persons with handicapping conditions to speak to the group. Or invite several people to participate in a panel discussion. You might invite a social worker, a special-education teacher, an agency director, a therapist, and an interpreter. Ask your guests to talk about their experiences and the rewards and challenges of their work.

Group Time: Planning for Ministry

Bring the youth together to discuss possibilities for ministry to persons with handicapping conditions. Emphasize that the youth will be involved in ministry *with*, not just ministry *to*, persons with handicapping conditions. A project in which the youth "do something nice for the handicapped" is not ministry; it is patronizing and offensive. The emphasis of ministry should be empowerment, encouragement, and affirmation of persons as persons. Group members may want to volunteer for the Special Olympics or at an agency or institution, or they may prefer to plan a weekend retreat for children with handicapping conditions. Invite the guest speakers to suggest possible projects.

✝ Closing Worship ✝

Hymns: Choose hymns or songs that speak about God's love and God's care for everyone.
Litany:Invite the youth to write their own litany from their experiences on this retreat.
Scripture: Consider using any of the following passages.

> **Psalm 27 or 41 or 91**
> **Romans 8**
> **Colossians 1:11-29**
> **Mark 5:21-43**
> **Luke 17:11-19**

Invite the youth to reflect on the meaning of these scripture passages for their life and for people they know.

Commitment:Provide an opportunity for youth to make a commitment to: help persons who are handicapped; work for accessibility in their church and/or community; be in ministry with children and youth who are living with handicapping conditions; help youth at school be more understanding toward persons with handicapping conditions.

Closing Hymn: "Here I Am, Lord"

—Grant Hagiya

Note: Youth who have experienced this retreat may want to consider surveying their church building or another public building to determine accessibility. This exercise can provide important data for the church and allow youth to become advocates for persons with handicapping conditions.

13

BUILDING A COMMUNITY OF TRUST

PURPOSE: *To help youth experience what it means to be the body of Christ as individuals participating in a community of love.*

Preparation

Divide the youth group into planning teams for meal preparation, recreation, recruitment of participants, transportation, and administration. Just doing the four sessions will take at least a Friday evening and a Saturday. Two full days would give you more time to complete the sessions and to relax and enjoy one another.

POSSIBLE SCHEDULE (3 days)

FRIDAY EVENING
   7:00 Gather, unpack
   7:30 Session 1: Getting started
        Part 1: Building a group
   8:30 Part 2: Getting started
   9:15 Group singing, storytelling
        Bonfire if weather permits

SATURDAY
   8:00 Morning devotions
   8:30 Breakfast
   9:00 Session 2: This is who we are
  10:30 Break
  11:00 Session 2 (cont.)
        Worship
  12:00 Lunch
   1:00 Session 3: This is who I am
   3:00 Group activities
   5:00 Dinner
        Free time
   7:00 Session 3 (cont.)
   8:30 Recreation
  10:00 Evening devotions

SUNDAY
   8:30 Breakfast
   9:00 Session 4: This is whose we are
        What promises has God made?
        What does it mean to say "God is
        love?" What does it mean to say "I
        believe?"
  10:00 Break
  10:30 Closing worship
        Holy Communion
  12:00 Lunch
        Head for home

SESSION 1: Getting Involved

Part 1: Building a Group.

1. Give a copy of the descriptions below to each member of the group. Group members are to find a person to fit each description and get his or her signature. Allow ten minutes for the activity.

Getting to Know Who

1. Is wearing red
2. Can stand on his or her (must demonstrate)
3. Like classical music
4. Has a pet cat
5. Woke up before 6:30 this morning
6. Can whistle the Doxology (must demonstrate)
7. Has a birthday this month
8. Likes math
9. Plays a sport on a school team
10. Can spell Youth Fellowship backwards (must demonstrate)
11. Is wearing a necklace
12. Worshiped at the church last Sunday

2. Cut sheets of 9-by-12-inch construction paper in 4½-by-6-inch pieces. Give each group member as many pieces of paper as there are letters in his or her first name. Invite persons to write each letter of their first name on a separate piece of paper. Have the group work together to create a crossword puzzle using all the first names. Begin with the longest name and arrange the other names horizontally or vertically so that some letters are part of two names. Tape all the letters together and tape the crossword to a wall.

3. Ask persons to imagine that the center of the room is the center of a bicycle wheel, that the walls are touched by the tire, and that the spokes run between the walls and the center of the room. Explain that the center of the wheel represents the core of the group, where persons feel they really belong to the group. Ask both youth and adults to stand at the spot on the wheel that represents how close they feel to the core of the group. Ask: In what ways have you felt important to the group? When have you felt left out?

4. Give the following instructions: Go to a person you do not know well and talk about your favorite TV shows for ninety-two seconds. With your partner, find another team and talk about favorite childhood memories for four minutes and six seconds.

5. Give each group of four a copy of the "Weird and Goofy Scavenger Hunt" on the next page. Tell them they have twenty minutes to collect as many items as possible.

TO SCAVENGER HUNT

Weird and Goofy Scavenger Hunt

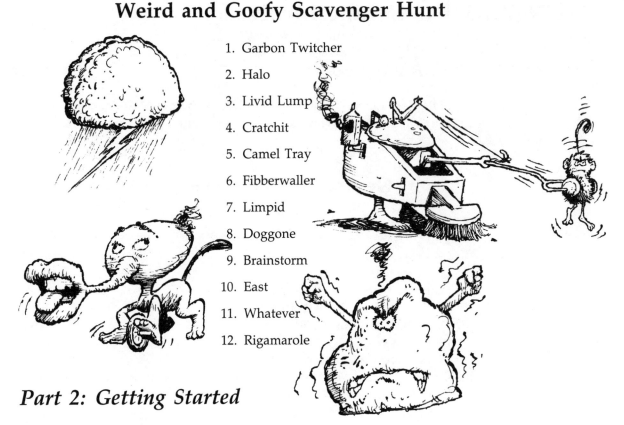

1. Garbon Twitcher
2. Halo
3. Livid Lump
4. Cratchit
5. Camel Tray
6. Fibberwaller
7. Limpid
8. Doggone
9. Brainstorm
10. East
11. Whatever
12. Rigamarole

Part 2: Getting Started

Gather the group together. Explain the purpose and outline of the event. Review the schedule, rules, and responsibilities.

Worship

Ask a group member to read **1 Corinthians 12:12-20.** Read aloud the following:

Look at your hands. Study them for a moment. *(Pause.)* Look at the lines in your hands. Think of the things your hands have done in the last week. How have you used your hands to work, to play, or to do something for someone else? *(Pause.)* God doesn't work in isolation. God depends on you. You are God's hands wherever you go and whatever you do. Think of ways in which you can be God's hands during the time we are together. Share your thoughts with God in silent prayer.

SESSION 2: This Is Who We Are

List the rules for an emotionally safe environment:

—It's OK to pass.
—I speak only for myself.
—I say only what's comfortable.
—Confidentiality is respected.

State the purpose of this session: to share three ingredients that help build trust and intimacy in a group—cooperating with one another rather than competing; working together, not alone; and recognizing each individual.

Divide into three groups and give each group one of the following assignments:

Read Acts 2:43-47. What does this Scripture say about cooperation? Have you ever seen people working together in similar ways? If so, what happened? Use your bodies to create a human sculpture describing what it means to be a cooperative group.

Read 1 Corinthians 12:14-20. What does the Scripture say about working together and working alone? Have you seen the meaning of this Scripture come true? If so, what happened? Create a song about working together using the tune of "Row, Row, Row Your Boat."

Read Luke 15:4-7. What does this Scripture say about the importance of each person? How have you seen the importance of this Scripture in the life of your youth group? Develop a skit about volleyball (or another team sport) that describes the theme of this Scripture.

When the teams have completed their assignments, come together as a group. Invite Group 1 to summarize their Scripture and discussion and present their sculpture. Allow time for discussion. Make two columns on chalkboard or paper. Title one column "Cooperative" and the other column "Competitive." Work together to list ways in which the group has been cooperative in recent months. Also, list ways in which group members have competed with one another. Review the lists. Ask this question: Are there things we can do to be even more cooperative than we have been in the past? Add any suggestions to the list.

Invite Group 2 to summarize their Scripture and discussion and to present their song. Allow time for discussion. Draw a large circle on the floor. Read a list of events or happenings that have taken place in the life of the group in the last few months. (Be as specific as possible.) After reading each item on the list, ask persons to stand inside the circle if they felt the group was working together in that event. Ask them to stand outside the circle if they felt someone was left out.

Invite Group 3 to summarize their Scripture and discussion and to present their skit. Allow time for discussion. Read the following situation:

Bobbi is an active member of your youth group. She was elected treasurer about three months ago. Tonight, in the middle of your meeting, Bobbi suddenly resigns as treasurer and leaves the room. You follow Bobbi out into the parking lot and ask, "What's wrong?" The answer surprises you: "This group is just a clique. Only a few people are important. The rest of us don't count. I'm leaving."

Ask these questions:

● Have you ever felt the way Bobbi felt?
● What would you say to her?
● Do you remember times when this group acted like a clique?
● What makes us feel that we are important to the group?
● What, if anything, needs to be done to make certain all persons feel included?

Spread sheets of newspaper around the floor and ask group members to tape the paper together so that it resembles a patchwork carpet. Make certain the finished creation is large enough that all persons can fit under it with room to spare. Ask persons to imagine the paper represents the group. The group is vitally important and must be held aloft. At no time should it be allowed to slip to the floor. Invite the youth to hold up the newspaper "rug" and stand under it, making certain it does not touch the floor. Then tell one or two persons at a time they are not needed under the paper and ask them to step aside. (At first, the people who are left will be able to hold up the paper, although with difficulty. Eventually, as more

persons are asked to leave, the burden will become too great. The paper will fall to the floor.)
Ask these questions: What does this exercise say about our group? What does it say about cooperation and competition? about working together, not alone? about the importance of the individual?

Worship

Invite group members to sit in a comfortable position. Read **I Corinthians 12:12-20.** Read the following:

Focus your attention on your eyes and ears. What do you see right now? What can you hear? What have you seen during this day? What have you heard? You are God's eyes and ears in this world. You have the ability to see life in a different way. You also have the opportunity to listen to the joys and hurts of your world. Think of ways you have been God's eyes and ears during the last week. Share your thoughts with God in silent prayer.

SESSION 3: This Is Who I Am

Explain that the purpose of this session is to allow individuals to explore who they are as God's special persons. Ask youth to sit in a circle. Ask each person to choose an animal, an automobile, and a color that say something about who he or she is. After reminding the group of the rules for a safe environment, invite the youth to share reasons for their choices.

Give each person a copy of the lifeline on this page. Then give the following instructions: Place an X on the horizontal line to indicate your age. Identify the major events in your life. Were they highs or lows? Draw wavy lines on your chart describing your life up to this point. Then imagine your life in the future. Complete the chart to age twenty-five.

When everyone has finished, invite individuals to share their lifeline with one other person.

My Lifeline

As High as
You Get

Birth————————————————————————— Age 25

As Low as
It Goes

When pairs have finished, draw the group together. Ask these questions: In general, do you feel positive or negative about your past? How do you feel about where you are right now? Are you more excited or frightened about your lifeline in the future?

Reprint the quotations below on separate sheets of paper. Ask the youth to choose a quotation that describes a feeling they have had. Then ask them to paint a picture describing what the statement means to them. (This painting could be a series of colors or shapes. It need not be a portrait.) As they complete their painting, instruct the youth to share their creation with two other people.

"I am surrounded by many troubles—too many to count!"
—David, in Psalm 40:42,TEV

"My God, my God, why have you abandoned me? I have cried desperately for help, but still it does not come."

—Psalm 22:1, TEV

"You are like light for the whole world."
—Jesus, in Matthew 5:14, TEV

"We are often troubled, but not crushed; sometimes in doubt, but never in despair."
—Paul, in II Corinthians 4:8, TEV

"Ask, and you will receive; seek, and you will find."
—Jesus, in Matthew 7:7, TEV

Ask persons to think of one thing about themselves of which they are proud. Ask them to be prepared to brag with others. Give persons the opportunity to share their brag one at a time. Instruct the group to give encouragement before and cheers after each person's contribution.

Place large construction paper cutouts of a circle, a square, and a triangle on the floor. Ask persons to stand by the shape that most closely represents how they feel about the group. Allow time for group members to explain the reasons for their decisions.

Worship

Invite group members to sit in a comfortable position. Read aloud **1 Corinthians 12:12-20.** Read the following:

Focus your attention on your mind. What have you been thinking during the last twenty-four hours? *(Pause.)* What decisions have you made? *(Pause.)* As you look ahead to the next year, what choices will you have to make? *(Pause.)* Being Christian means making choices. You live your faith in the hundreds of decisions you make every day. As you think and as you decide, God's mind is in you. Share some of your thoughts with God in silent prayer.

SESSION 4: This Is Whose We Are

Explain that persons will have the opportunity during this time to consider their relationship with God. They will read Scripture, discuss its meaning for their lives, and find ways to share their discoveries with the rest of the group in worship.

Introduce three areas for exploration: What promises has God made? What does it mean to say "God is love"? What does it mean to say "I believe"? Divide into three interest areas, and give each group the appropriate information on the next page.

Scripture Study

What Promises Has God Made?
Scripture: Jeremiah 31:33; Matthew 28:19-20; Revelation 21:5-7
- What do these verses say about God's promises?
- Do you think these promises are helpful to youth? Why or why not?
- How will you share your thoughts and feelings with the rest of the group in worship?

What Does it Mean to Say "God Is Love"?
Scripture: Matthew 27:45-54; Ephesians 2:8-9; Psalm 23:1-3
- In your opinion, what do these verses say about God's love?
- What do these verses say to you personally?
- What questions would you like to ask the writers of these verses?
- How will you share your thoughts and feelings with the rest of the group in worship?

What Does It Mean to Say "I Believe"?
Scripture: Matthew 16:13-16; Romans 5:1; I John 1:5-7
- What are the most important things these verses are saying to you?
- What does it mean to you to say "I believe"?
- How will you share your thoughts and feelings with the rest of the group in worship?

†   Closing Worship   †

When all three groups have finished planning, share the worship experiences they have created. Close by gathering in a tight circle and holding one another close. Ask persons to offer sentence prayers describing their feelings about their experiences during their time together.

—Larry F. Beman

14

THE COMPLETE YOUTH GROUP CHECKUP

PURPOSE: *To help youth and leaders remember their identity as the body of Christ, check up on their group life, define a health youth group, set group and personal goals.*

This planning retreat is an interactive drama using extemporaneous dialogue and simple medical jargon and props to help youth take stock of the health of their group. As retreat leader, you will guide the drama. You will need to be familiar with this program guide.

Preparation

A month in advance, divide youth into work groups: (1) Props/Scenes will prepare signs to label scenes and arrange donations or loans of medical props. (2) Menus/Meals will work with a licensed dietician to plan tasty, easy-to-prepare meals and snacks that model healthy nutrition for teens. (3) Invitations/Publicity will prepare and post fliers and posters about the retreat, write newsletter articles, mail invitations and permission slips to all youth, and arrange telephone calls to inactive youth. (4) Fitness/Exercise will ask a fitness instructor to teach an adult and several teens some simple stretching and aerobics routines using popular teen music. Exercise will be used for five-minute and ten-minute breaks.

POSSIBLE SCHEDULE (2 days)

SATURDAY
  9:00 Arrive
  9:30 Make name tags, Game A
10:00 Opening worship
10:15 Scenes 1, 2, 3
12:30 Lunch, recreation
  5:00 Supper
  5:30 Scenes 4, 5
  7:45 Informal music, Game B
  8:30 Scene 6
  9:45 Game C, movie, table games, informal music
11:30 Devotions
12:00 Lights out

SUNDAY
  8:00 Rise, breakfast
  9:00 Closing worship
10:15 Leave for home
11:45 Arrive at church

Game A

Give each youth a pencil and a photocopy of instructions to get autographs of youth who:

1. go to the same doctor they do
2. ever had an operation
3. ever had a cast for a broken bone
4. take regular medication
5. ever stayed overnight in a hospital
6. had the chicken pox
7. had a medical checkup in the last year
8. have a family member working in the medical field
9. ever had their blood pressure checked
10. know how to read a mercury thermometer.

Opening Worship

Tell the group the purpose of the retreat: to evaluate your youth ministry, to find out what a healthy youth group is like, and to set goals and make plans for the group. Read **Romans 12**, which describes a Christian community. Sing together "Spirit of the Living God."

Explain the format of the retreat and that youth are to interact with the "doctor" and others as directed.

Scene 1: Medical School

Scenario: The retreat leader, wearing a lab coat and a doctor name tag, is in a "Medical School Lecture Hall," teaching medical students (all the youth) the qualities and structure of a healthy youth group in the body of Christ. The leader will present a portrait of a balanced, vital youth ministry, which includes service, worship, fellowship, study, and outreach. In advance, prepare charts or posters of the main points for youth to focus on and to refer to later when treatment options are discussed. Following the lecture, lead five minutes of stretching and aerobics before moving to the next scene.

Scene 2: At the Doctor's Office

Scenario: A counselor leads the youth wearing the Body of Christ name tag to a door labeled "Doctor's Office," reassuring the Body of Christ that the checkup won't hurt, that it's just to find out if the body is healthy or needs treatments, prescriptions, and so on. The counselor and Body go to the "Waiting Room." Another counselor, who is wearing a nurse's cap, asks Body to complete the first page of a medical chart (a large newsprint pad on an easel). With help from all the youth, Body fills in the church or group name, the address, the age range of youth in the group, the number of females and males in the group, the racial make-up, and so on.

Scene 3: Examination Room

Scenario: Nurse calls Body into the "Examination Room," where Body sits on a sheet-draped table. Doctor conducts a medical checkup by asking questions that all youth and counselors help answer in order to evaluate the youth program. Nurse writes the answers on a large newsprint pad to use in later sessions.

Question 1

Doctor checks Body's height and weight with a bathroom scale and a yardstick and asks Nurse to record statistics about the size of the youth group, increases or losses since last year, known reasons for gains or losses, and so on. (Research these figures ahead of time and give the information to Doctor to tell Nurse.)

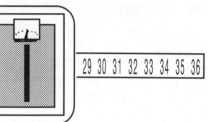

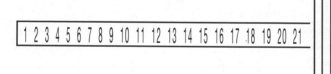

Question 2

Doctor checks the temperature of Body with a thermometer while asking the youth group questions to find out if they think the group is cold or warm (determined by how youth and leaders treat members, inactives, and visitors and by whether the activities and the environment are warm and caring or cold and cliquish).

Question 3

Doctor checks Body's blood pressure while asking questions of the group to find out if the group's blood pressure is high (because of too much going on, no balance in program, not enough adult support); low (because of the youth group's invisibility or ineffectiveness); or normal (because of a balanced program, good support, involvement and visibility in church and community).

Question 4

Doctor conducts an examination of Body's eyes, ears, nose, and throat with a flashlight and a tongue depressor and asks group members if their vision of the Christian faith as revealed in the Bible is cloudy or clear; if they hear God's "still small voice" in the midst of their activities and fellowship; if the fragrance of their offerings of time, talent, and money is pleasing to God; and if their voices are a witness for God.

Question 5

Doctor listens to Body's heart with a stethoscope and asks questions to find out if the group's heart is:

- skipping beats—missing chances for service; ignoring visitors; mis-scheduling regular and special programs
- beating too fast—wearing out youth, leaders, and parents with too many activities, poor planning, or too many fund-raisers; being too busy with recreation and leaving no time for worship or study
- sluggish—doing too little to forge group identity; placing too little emphasis on spiritual growth opportunities
- normal—maintaining a balanced program so that all parts of the body are nourished and built up

Question 6

Doctor checks Body's reflexes and joint flexibility while asking about the group's prayer and worship life. (Does the group plan meaningful, youth-oriented worship? kneel together at the church altar? share prayer concerns in the group or with the prayer chain?)

Question 7

Doctor asks about Body's diet to see if it is balanced and nourishing or if it includes too many empty calories and too much junk food. (Does the group have a balanced program? How do school, sports, family and community activities fit in? Do programs nourish growth in faith? Are programs empty of meaning or only for fun?)

Question 8

Doctor asks about Body's exercise program to see if the youth group is active and moving, exercising its purpose and realizing its potential. (How does the youth group live out its purpose? Does the group flex its spiritual muscles? Does it carry the weight of servanthood?)

Question 9

Doctor examines an X-ray and discusses the skeletal system that is essential to support a healthy body of Christ. (Do parents, church and youth leaders, the organization and structure of the youth fellowship offer effective support? Do they promote growth and strength or break down easily?)

Scene 4: Doctor's Office

Scenario: In an area labeled "Doctor's Office," Doctor meets with Body to discuss the findings of the checkup. All the youth and counselors will participate in this doctor-patient conference by responding to the leader's observations about how to treat problem areas and how to keep healthy areas functioning well. Review medical chart notes from Scenes 2 and 3 (posted on the wall), and compare your youth group's program and structure to the model of a healthy, fully functioning youth group presented in Scene 1. Also reread Romans 12 and design a general plan for good health. Set a timetable for treatments, ranking those that need immediate attention and those that are longer-term goals. Divide youth and counselors into small groups to work as "medical teams" in the next session. Break for ten minutes of stretching and aerobics.

Scene 5: Hospital

Scenario: Small groups will meet as medical teams to come up with specific plans to treat the problems they are assigned. Later, in Scene 6, the teams will present their plans to the whole group by acting out the treatment they choose, using medical props and terms.

Before medical teams meet, remind them of the "lecture notes" and "medical chart" and show them the props. Give some examples:

1. Operate to cut out unnecessary programs, uncaring attitudes, and superficial prayers. (Props could be white sheets, surgical gowns and masks, disposable gloves, kitchen tongs and table knives.)
2. Transplant a lung (balloon) to symbolize the breath of the Holy Spirit in new worship experiences or Bible study, or transplant a heart (cut-out red construction paper heart) to add a summer work project to the calendar.
3. Bandage (with bandage strips or gauze) a still-tender wound caused by the resignation of a well-loved youth leader and write a prescription for an immediate series of programs on the stages of grief.
4. Present a food-groups chart to show a balanced youth fellowship diet of fellowship and recreation, study, worship, and service. Also present monthly menus to suggest specific ways to keep the program balanced.
5. Design a program of exercising faith by running errands for older adults and by lifting babies in the church nursery. (Use light weights, jogging shoes, sweatbands, and so on.)
6. Immunize (with toy hypodermic syringes) against the epidemic of spiritual apathy with a study on prayer and weekly boosters of altar time during youth vespers.

Game B

For this game, you will need a bathroom scale, a yardstick, a blood pressure kit, someone to check blood pressure, and another to check heart rates. Divide into groups of four (1) to check blood pressure of each youth and to add together diastolic and systolic pressures of all to get the combined blood pressure of group; (2) to measure the height of each youth in inches and to add the inches together for a combined group height; (3) to check the resting heart rate of each youth and to add all the heart rates together; (4) to check heart rates for each youth after he or she has run in place for two minutes and to add all the youth's heart rates together; (5) to find out the total height in inches of each of the other groups and, with the other groups, to arrange themselves in a line from the tallest to the shortest group.

Scene 6: Hospital

Youth medical teams act out their treatment plans, using medical jargon and props. Be sure youth announce the health problems they are treating. Consider videotaping this segment. Nurse records all treatment plans on the medical chart (a newsprint pad on an easel) for later reference.

Game C

Youth and counselors sit in a large circle. "It" is in the middle and has the task of choosing someone in the circle and trying to make him or her smile or laugh by saying: "Smile, Baby, I think I love ya!" The person chosen must respond without smiling or laughing: "I love ya, Baby, but I just can't smile." If the person chosen smiles or laughs, he or she becomes "It."

Evening Devotions

In a darkened room, hold candles or flashlights, sing "Kum Ba Yah."

Invite youth to go quietly outside with flashlights for a brief silent walk together or to sit in a group where they can see the sky.

After the walk and while youth are still outside, play a cassette tape of someone singing, "Creator of the Stars of Night." After a period of silence, close with a unison reading of the prayer "For a Peaceful Night."

† Closing Worship †

Invite youth to offer prayers of hope for the new day.

Sing responsively "This Is the Day the Lord Has Made."

Sing together "This Is My Father's World".

Read **Romans 12.**

Ask youth to review the plans they have made at the retreat and to tell what they most look forward to in the coming year. Ask how they will personally contribute to the health of the body of Christ.

Sing together "God Be with You till We Meet Again"

—Susan C. Williams

15

MORE THAN JUST A GAME

PURPOSE: *To help the youth discover that the purpose of the youth group goes beyond recreation and fellowship.*

Almost everyone enjoys a good game, and your youth fellowship is probably no exception. This event centers around a variety of games and will help your group have fun and build a sense of community. The event will also help your members realize that the Christian life is more than just a game, and that youth group has a purpose that extends beyond simply having a good time. The event uses games to help you discover exactly what your group's purpose might be.

Preparation

Read through the retreat directions carefully ahead of time. Each activity lists the supplies needed. Decide which games and activities you want to include and then gather the needed materials. Be sure to include the youth in your decisions.

POSSIBLE SCHEDULE (Lock-In)

FRIDAY NIGHT

8:30 P.M.	Play active games:	12:40 A.M.	Play Can-You-Remember?
9:30	Play Personal Password		Charades
10:05	A Worshipful Moment #1	12:55	A Worshipful Moment #3
10:10	Break refreshments	1:00	Break; snacks
10:40	Paper airplane throwing contest	1:30	Flashlight Treasure Hunt
		2:00	Get Down to Work
11:00	Play the Name Game	2:30	A Worshipful Moment #4
11:15	A Worshipful Moment #2	2:35	Play board & card games, watch movies, sleep(?)
11:20	Play Ping-Pong Hockey		
12:00	Play Purpose Pictionary	7:00	Eat breakfast; head for home

Directions for Activities

Personal Password

Purpose: to identify the "make-up" of your group—who are your members, and what are their personal interests and values.

Supplies needed: index cards, pencils, stopwatch or timer, large sheets of paper, felt-tip markers.

Give each participant an index card and pencil. Ask him or her to write down on the card a word or phrase that describes himself or herself or an interest or value that he or she holds. (Examples: a member who loves music might write down "Singing"; another might list "Adventuresome"; another person might write down "Justice" if that is something he or she values). Do not let anyone see what is written on the card.

Divide the group into two teams and play Password with the words on these cards, using the following procedure:

- Choose a person to serve as the first game show host or M.C. The word on that person's card is the word to be guessed during this round.
- Each team will send one member to the front, and the M.C. will show the persons what is written on the card.
- The game now begins. The person from the first team gives a one-word clue which is a synonym of the word on the card; her team has 15 seconds to try to guess the word. If they miss, the person from the second team gives a one-word clue, and his team has 15 seconds to try to guess the word. Play stops after five clues have been given. Points are awarded as follows:

> correct guess with 1 clue—10 points
> correct guess with 2 clues—8 points
> correct guess with 3 clues—6 points
> correct guess with 4 clues—4 points
> correct guess with 5 clues—2 points

When the word has been guessed (or revealed), the M.C. writes that word down on a large sheet of paper labeled: Our Personal Interests and Values. Post this list where everyone can see it.

Continue playing in the same manner until everyone's word has been added to the list.

At the conclusion of the game, discuss this list. Do you feel it is a good description of your members? Were many words or ideas duplicated? What do these words say about your group? Add any additional words to the list that you feel are needed to provide a realistic picture of your members' interests and values.

A Worshipful Moment #1:

Purpose: to celebrate the importance of each individual in the group.

Ask each person to get a partner.

Turn to your partner, look into his/her eyes, and complete this sentence: "I am glad you are a part of our Youth Fellowship because _____ ."

Then, take a moment in silent prayer for your partner
—Thank God for him/her.
—Thank God for this person's special interests, values, and abilities.
—Ask God to help your group to be especially meaningful and helpful for your partner in the coming year.

The Name Game

Purpose: to help participants think about the kinds of persons they would like to be as Christians—what does it mean to have the name "Christian?"

Supplies needed: paper, pencils, large sheets of paper, felt-tip markers.

Divide into groups, with three persons per team. Give each person on the team a piece of paper and a pencil.

First, have all three team members print their names on the top of all three sheets. (Each participant will have three names on his/her sheet.) Decide as a group whether you will use full names, or first and last names only.

Then, working individually, the participants will have 3 minutes to use the letters on the top of their sheet to spell words that describe the kinds of people they would like to be as Christians. Include words that show what a Christian might be or do. Words may be adjectives, nouns, verbs—any part of speech is OK, but do not use proper nouns. Words must be spelled correctly in order to count; any single letter can be used only once per word. (Example: names on the top of a sheet might be David Nelson, Monica Lopez, and Michael Kissinger. Words that could be spelled from those letters might include kind, loving, caring, serve, helper, and so on.)

The winner from each group is the person who can spell the largest number of words within three minutes.

Then, have each team compile a list of all of the words their members have found. (Do not count duplicated words.) Write this list on a large sheet of paper labeled "The Kind of People We Would Like To Be," and post this list where everyone can see it. The team with the longest list wins.

A Worshipful Moment #2:

Purpose: to help participants identify areas in which they would like to grow as Christians. Have the participants remain in their small groups.

Ask each person to look at the lists "The Kind of People We Would Like To Be," and to think about his or her own relationship with God. Ask each one to consider the areas in which he feels he still needs some personal or spiritual growth. Each person will choose one word from the list and share that word with his small group. (For example: "I get angry with people and stay angry—I would like to be more forgiving.")

Then, have each team spend a few moments in prayer for the persons on that team, asking God's help for the specific needs that have just been mentioned.

Conclude by singing one verse of *Lord, I Want to be a Christian in My Heart*.

Pictionary

Purpose: to encourage members to think about possible goals and purposes for a youth group.

Supplies needed: Chalkboard and chalk or large sheets of paper and felt-tip markers, stop-watch or timer, prepared word cards.

Divide into two teams. Give one member of the first team a word card. On this card will be a word or phrase that describes a possible goal or purpose for a youth group. That person will have 2 minutes to draw clues so that his or her team can correctly guess the phrase. Only pictures (no numbers or words) may be used. If the team can correctly identify the phrase within 2 minutes, they will get 2 points. If they cannot guess it, the other team will have 1 minute to try. (One of their members looks at the word card, and draws a sketch.) If the second team can identify the word, they will get 1 point.

Continue playing, using the rest of the word cards. Have the teams take turns being the first to draw.

Suggested words and phrases might be:

Group Building	Bible Study
Fund-Raising	Service
Fellowship	Recreation
Spiritual Growth	Eating
Have Fun	Learn to Pray
Learn New Skills	Singing
Go Camping	Ski Trips
Discuss Christian Issues	Worship
Gaining Self-Understanding	Make Friends
Have an Uplifting Experience	

As each phrase is guessed, write it down on a list entitled: "Possible Purposes for a Youth Group." Post this list where everyone can see it.

At the conclusion of the game, discuss this list. List any additional goals and purposes that a youth group might have. Then, go through this entire list and set priorities for the items as you see them relating to the purposes and goals of your youth group. Number them in order of importance.

"Can-You-Remember?" Charades

Purpose: to celebrate past events and activities and their value to your group.

Divide into four teams, and assign each team one of your group's top four goals and purposes (as determined at the conclusion of Purpose Pictionary). Ask each team to think back over the past year's activities and to select the one activity they believe best fulfilled that particular goal or purpose. Pantomime that activity and see if the other groups can guess the event you are recalling.

Spend some time reminiscing about those special activities and why they were meaningful and successful.

A Worshipful Moment #3:

Purpose: to thank God for working through your group during the past year.

Stand in a large circle, either with your arms around each other's shoulders or holding hands. Have one person read **Colossians 1:3-8** out loud. Then, have a circle prayer. Go around the circle, giving prayers of thanks to God for the way your group has been able to show faith and love in the past year.

Down to Work

Purpose: to evaluate your group's past program and to project future events and activities.
Supplies needed: paper, pencils, large sheets of paper, felt-tip markers.

Make a list of as many of last year's activities as you can remember. Include regular activities, study topics, special projects, trips, parties, fund raisers, retreats, service projects—everything. (It would be even better if the leader would hand out a printed list of these events, and then the group could make additions.)

Using the lists made earlier ("Our Personal Interests and Values," "The Kind of People We Would Like To Be," and "Possible Purposes for a Youth Group"), analyze the events of the past year:

- What was the basic purpose of each activity?
- Did you meet most/all/few of your group's major purposes and goals?
- Did you provide activities that fit the interests of most/all/few of your members?
- Did you have a good balance of activities or was too much time spent on some kinds of events?
- How did your activities help group members in the area of spiritual growth—were there opportunities to help persons become "the kind of people we would like to be"?
- What were your greatest disappointments?
- Which of last year's activities do you want to repeat this year?

Take some time to brainstorm possible activities for the coming year. Try to fill in any gaps that currently exist in meeting the purposes, interests, and needs of your group.

Directions for Additional Games

Paper Airplane Throwing Contest

Supplies needed: old church bulletins (or other paper).

Go to the sanctuary of the church. Give each person an old church bulletin, or other piece of paper, which he or she will fold into a paper airplane. Stand in the back of the sanctuary, or in the balcony, if there is one. Throw the airplanes, aiming at the target—which is the pastor's pulpit! (If you pastor is available and willing, he or she could be standing in the pulpit during the competition.) Be sure to pick up all the paper when you are finished.

Ping Pong Hockey

Supplies needed: ping pong balls, old newspapers, masking tape, two tables.

Divide into two teams. Give each person several sheets of newspaper. Roll the sheets lengthwise into a tight tube, and tape them. These newspaper tubes will serve as the hockey sticks.

Set the tables on their sides to serve as the goals. Make sure that the tables are well-balanced, so that they will not fall over. The top of the table should face the playing area. Assign one person from each team to be the goalie.

To play the game, teams will attempt to hit the hockey puck (a ping pong ball) against their goal, using the newspaper tubes. The goalie may use any part of his or her body to keep the ball from hitting the table, but the other players may touch the ball only with their sticks.

Flashlight Treasure Hunt

Supplies needed: flashlights, a treasure (a prize of some sort), slips of papers with clues written on them.

Hide the treasure and the clues.

Divide into teams. Give each team a flashlight. Participants search for clues in the dark, using only the light from the flashlight.

✝   Closing Worship   ✝

Purpose: to encourage the group's commitment to one another and to God.
Supplies needed: candle, matches
Light a candle, and set it in the worship area.
Read **Matthew 5:31-4.** Challenge the group to accept the task of being salt and light to one another and to the world around us. Then pray, asking God's guidance and support for your group during the coming year. Close by singing a favorite song.

—Rhoda Preston